Tunisia

Jarrold Publishing

CONTENTS

Sunset

This is Tunisia

The words 'Holiday in Africa' will probably immediately conjure up for some dreams of herds of elephants and packs of lions on the Serengeti, for others broad deserts with sandstorms, flashing Arab stallions, wild Bedouin sheiks and dangerous meetings at the wells of the oases.

In that respect, Tunisia, the most easterly of the three North African Atlas countries, will definitely disappoint you; long gone are the days when this country in the Maghreb (the Arab West) used to deliver lions and leopards for the Roman gladiator contests. Today, in the north, apart from numerous birds the principal wildlife is wild boar, whilst that in the south consists of the rarely seen dainty gazelles, desert foxes and jackals, while the only adventures to be found are harmless flirting on the golden sands or camel rides under the palm crests of the oases.

So things are rather different from the over-imaginative descriptions of the previous century. Nevertheless, anyone who makes the three- or four-hour air trip from Great Britain to Tunisia will find that he has landed in a different and strange world. The modernisation of life during the last three decades, the emancipation of young women who have cast aside the veil, the introduction of the motor car in the place of ass and camel have erased many picturesque features from the face of Tunisia, but have not destroyed them. Behind the battlemented walls of the old towns, the *medinas*, in the covered streets of the bazaars, the *souks*, in the unique silhouettes of the minarets, in the domes of the holy sepulchres, the *marabouts*, and in the giant fortresses, the *ribats*, the Orient paints its unchanging and fascinating pictures.

Nun-like women in white veils, Bedouins in multi-coloured clothes bedecked with silver jewellery, carrying on their backs pots filled with water from the stream, men in blue cloaks riding their asses, or the winding silhouettes of long camel caravans — these are aspects of a strange and mysteriously alluring world which will have a special effect on every visitor.

However, this world is not to be found in the carpeted halls and the shady palm-gardens of the hotels, or on the well kept beaches. You must tear yourself away from those if you wish to find the magic of the East in this age-old land of culture.

A land for exploration

There are places to be discovered just about everywhere in Tunisia and — since the country is not big — they can be reached from almost all holiday centres on a one- or two-day excursion. Here you can walk in the tracks of the Romans in Carthage, Dougga, Bulla Regia, Thuburbo Majus, Maktar, Sbeitla or El Djem. You can visit Kairouan, the Holy City of Islam, which was for a long time closed to non-believers, and further south you may be enticed by the mysterious desert with its oases, by the cave-dwellings of Matmata, the refuges and castles of Médenine and by the great salt lake of Chott El Djerid, on the southern bank of which the Sahara finally begins.

Anyone who prefers to drive himself rather than join an organised tour must be able to adapt to the particular driving style of the Tunisians — this is governed more by temperament and fatalism than by any traffic regulations. The traffic on the country roads is less chaotic than in the larger towns. The road network is well constructed and — with the exception of the tracks in the south — can be used by any car; road signs are in the French language. However, problems can occur after heavy falls of rain, mostly in winter and spring, when the dried-up rivers are suddenly filled with water again and the roads which pass through them are flooded. If you do not expect too much you will be able to find acceptable accommodation without difficulty. Hotels in the interior are improving.

Left: Dougga
Above: Mosque in Kairouan
Right: Thuburbo Majus

Essential details in brief

Name:
Al Djoumbouria Attunusia, République Tunisienne (Tunisian Republic).

Independence:
Since March 20th 1956.

Territory:
164,000 sq. km — 125,000 sq. km excluding the disputed area on the Libyan border. (Great Britain: 315,030 sq. km.)
Maximum distance north-south: 750 km.
Maximum distance east-west: 300 km.
1200 km of coastline.

Population:
7.7 million comprising:
Arabs and Berbers with small European minority (French, Italians, Maltese).

Growth rate:
2.5% per annum.

Population density:
46 per sq. km; Tunis (city) 2238 per sq. km; Gouvernorat of Médenine 34 per sq. km. (Great Britain: 228 per sq. km.),

Language:
State language Arabic; educational and commercial language French. Berber dialects still spoken by 3%.

Religion:
The State religion is Islam; 96% Muslims, mostly Sunnites. Small Christian and Jewish groups.

Form of Government:
Presidential Republic.

Head of State:
Zíne El Abedine Ben Ali who in 1987 replaced, owing to infirmity, Habib Bourguiba who had ruled for 30 years.

Representation of the people:
Single-chamber Parliament with 136 members.

Administrative structure:
23 districts (Gouvernorats).

Important exports:
Crude oil, phosphates, textiles, olive oil, wine, fruit.

Vital imports:
Machinery, motor vehicles, yarn, iron, steel, wheat, chemicals.

Important trading partners:
EEC countries, United States of America, Algeria, Saudi Arabia.

Bedouin

Village life

The Tunisian way of life

Everything in Tunisia revolves around the SMIG and the SMAG; these are the legally guaranteed minimum wages which are negotiated each year in hard rounds of discussions between the trades unions, the employers' union and the government. SMAG is the daily rate in agriculture (about 3 dinars per day) and SMIG applies to all other branches of commerce. For a 46-hour week a worker who is paid in accordance with SMIG will take home some 130 dinars (about £80) a month, including all extras (travel allowances, luncheon money, attendance bonus, etc.).

Higher up the scale things are better. A departmental manager in the state administration will get a monthly salary of about 550 dinars (£360), and life is also sweetened by other perks; an expense allowance, cheap housing and private use of the official car are the norm. As regards cars the cheapest small French car assembled in Tunisia costs about 8000 dinars (£4970). Imported cars attract customs duty, depending on their size, of between 150 and 400%. Consequently, for most Tunisians owning their own car is an unattainable dream; scarcely 9.5% of Tunisian households have a car of their own. However, you would be surprised at how many luxury cars are driven by the upper-middle class in Tunisia.

The average Tunisian household is made up of 5 or 6 people and when, as is often the case, there is only one wage-earner, then the subsistence level is reached all too quickly. For life in Tunisia is not cheap — with the exception of some basic foods such as bread, sugar and oil. All others, vegetables, meat and fish, are expensive for Tunisian income levels, and imported 'luxury' goods, which form part of normal living standards in Europe, are extremely dear. The price of whisky and brandy starts at 37 dinars (£23) per bottle. However, a Tunisian Muslim should have no interest in such

Douz camel-riders

Embroidery, Cap Bon

things, as the Prophet Mohammed forbade it!

Since the days of the Vandals the rumour has persisted that it is hot in North Africa. The summer tourist may indeed find it so, but in the winter months in the north of the country, which is also the most heavily populated, the thermometer seldom climbs above 15 degrees and as a result the houses become quite cool. The fact is that the heating period for houses in the north-east of Tunisia begins in November, and lasts until April. Naturally building construction takes due account of this. About 90% of all dwellings can be considered permanent buildings of which, however, only just over a third contain more than two rooms. The provision of 'home comforts' is still in its infancy in Tunisia; about 30% of dwellings have a kitchen with water laid on, and a bathroom or washroom is a rarity, only 13% of all houses having them. Properly installed cookers (47.5%) and refrigerators (31%) are not part of the normal furnishings — whereas the television is, every second family being thus kept in touch with world events.

Modernisation — a lengthy process

The blame for these remarkable figures lies primarily with the truly medieval conditions in the countryside, where being connected to the public drinking water and electricity supplies is very much the exception. It will be a long time yet before the romantic picture of women balancing water pitchers on their heads between stream and house becomes a thing of the past, since almost half of the Tunisian population still lives in the countryside. However, the move to the towns is unstoppable and the building industry is continually developing. The scale of new buildings extends from the magnificent neo-Moorish villas in the coastal suburbs of Tunis to two-roomed flats in social housing complexes at prices of 8000 dinars (£4970) upwards.

Those who can afford to do so build their own houses, sometimes taking years to do it by their own labour. The most important feature is a wall around the house high enough to avoid being overlooked. What goes on behind it is nobody else's business. What strikes one about modern Tunisian architecture is the move away from French influence and more and more towards the old Moorish style.

The small family does indeed exist in Tunisia, especially in the large towns, but normally a Tunisian lives in a large family with at least three generations living under one roof. This provides protection in many domestic situations, thus forming a sort of social network, but also demands adherence to traditions. Thus, for example, it is unimaginable that an unmarried woman should have a child, and if it does happen then she is, in practice, forced to hand the child over into the care of the state.

'Women's Lib'

In its legislation surrounding marriage and the family the Tunisian State is comparatively European; Mohammedan polygamy is not allowed and divorce is no longer the exclusive right of the husband, as it is in other Arab-Islamic states. Tunisian girls have the same educational opportunities as the men and a walk through the university campus in Tunis will show that they make good use of them.

They have dispensed with the *sefsari*, the white cloak which must cover all parts of the body from head to foot, and are moving towards French and Italian fashions. To pay for these Tunisian women also work — in factories, offices and commerce — self-confident and skilful. To a small degree they are also breaking away from the all too narrow confines of the family, and very gradually this is even happening in the mountain valleys and the cave dwellings.

Kairouan

How the Tunisians make a living

The Tunisian economy rests on very solid foundations, and energy costs, the biggest problem for most countries of the world, cause the Tunisians few headaches. They produce sufficient crude oil for domestic use and enjoy very good export earnings. Tunisia also possesses extensive phosphate deposits. Phosphate is a base constituent in fertiliser production, and is also exported. Tourism provides additional income and finally the Central Bank obtains currency through remittances from Tunisian workers abroad. Foreign currency is essential to Tunisia because the dinar is a purely internal currency and is not freely convertible into other currencies.

Agriculture

With such sources of income Tunisia would be able to run its economy very well were it not for its great problem, agriculture. Today Tunisia has to import over 50% of its food requirements, corn in particular, and also meat. Those interested in history may well ask how that can be the case, because the province of *Africa Proconsularis,* which roughly covered the present country of Tunisia, was once the granary of Rome.

The recession in agricultural production cannot be laid at the door of present-day Tunisia, rather it is the unavoidable consequence of a development which has taken place over a long period. In Roman times between 2.5 and 4 million people lived in Tunisia. Today there are about 7.7 million in the same area and the population is growing by 2.5% every year. There is a second and decisive reason why no comparison can be made with the granary of Roman times: the area suitable for agriculture has been constantly reducing over the past 2000 years. Erosion by water and wind and the apparently inexorable advance of the Sahara have destroyed huge areas of field and pasture. In the south they have tried to halt the advance of the Sahara by means of an artificial green belt, and in the north they are hoping to harness water by means of reservoirs. It is an almost hopeless war against the forces of nature where far too many battles are lost. So Tunisia has to spend its expensive foreign currency on importing food and is, therefore, unable to expand its industry.

Economic progress

In the terms of those providing development aid, Tunisia is one of the expanding countries which have progressed quite well economically. The national debt is being kept in check, and above all Arab capital is being invested in Tunisia by the wealthy men of the Gulf. In spite of that, however, industry is not expanding rapidly enough to provide sufficient jobs for the young. The rapid population growth has meant that the average age in Tunisia today is 20. It would need about 60,000 more jobs each year to provide work for the young and there is no chance of achieving that. As a result Tunisia exports its surplus work force to France and Italy. However, those countries have their own unemployment problems. To help alleviate these problems in the labour market the Tunisian government passed an Export Industry Law in 1972 which allows foreign firms to produce goods for the European market in Tunisia under customs licence. The advantages for the firms concerned are cheap Tunisian labour and relief from tax there; and for Tunisia — well over 30,000 jobs.

In addition the Ministry for the Economy is trying to set up 'joint ventures', i.e. the formation of a joint undertaking comprising a foreign company in partnership with a

Tunisian firm. However, this is not as simple as it sounds because the Tunisians insist on a majority shareholding in such ventures, wishing to remain masters in their own house. It remains to be seen whether they can so persuade the large European concerns.

Tunisia, of course, also suffers from world economic problems; to boost exports and declining tourism the Tunisian government devalued the dinar by almost 50% between 1984 and 1986. This made holidays in this interesting country less expensive for Europeans.

Tunisia and Islam

'Come to prayer, O ye faithful...' In Tunisia you cannot fail to hear the muezzin calling from the minaret, as he does throughout the Arab-Islamic world. However, Islam in Tunisia (and in Algeria and Morocco) is less uninhibited than in the east of the Arab world. One seldom sees a believer spreading out his prayer mat in public at the hour of prayer, whereas in Cairo or further east this is taken for granted. There, as a foreigner, you can enter almost any mosque, but in Tunisia it is frowned upon, even though the famous mosques at Kairouan or Tunis are open to tourists at certain times outside the hours of prayer. During the Ramadan month of fasting many cafés and restaurants may in fact stay open, especially in the tourist regions and the large towns, but only for foreigners.

Marabouts

Islam has deep roots in Tunisia and during the hundred years of French rule it formed a unifying bond for the people against the colonial masters. Finally, in Tunisia — as in the rest of the Maghreb — in addition to pure Islam, a kind of popular religion has developed, in which all kinds of village saints are revered, the so-called marabouts. As particularly devout men they were consulted during their lifetimes for advice on all aspects of life. Their burial mosques are scattered everywhere in the countryside. The wise men of Islam in the Al-Azhar University of Cairo or in Mecca do not recognise such deviations from pure strict Islam, but they tolerate them. 'Islam is a religion, nothing more and nothing less than a religion...' you will often hear Tunisians say, but this assertion leaves you with the uncertainty: is Islam truly only a religion? The strict Muslim cannot escape the fact that the Koran is also a book of law with rules on family law, criminal law and economic law. The rules of the Koran are today incorporated into the laws of many Arab-Islamic states. In Tunisia the law is largely orientated towards that of France.

That may prove very important in the future, for the wave of the Islamic revival movement is also spreading to Tunisia. What are known in the east of the Arab world as the Muslim Brotherhoods are the Integrists in the Maghreb. In Tunisia the *Mouvement de Tendence Islamique* has become established, though it does not enjoy recognition as a political party. The reason for that is that a policy of re-Islamisation conflicts with the efforts of the government to make Tunisia into a modern state orientated towards western meritocracy. This dispute is growing in Tunisia and no end can be seen to it.

Other religious beliefs no longer play any part in Tunisia. Admittedly, Christian services are still held regularly in Tunis Cathedral, but they are almost exclusively for a small European community.

13

🗿 Signposts of History

13th c. B.C: Phoenician seafarers from Asia Minor establish trading centres in North Africa and found Utica in 1101.

About 814: Founding of Carthage (Roman Punis) which through trade becomes a great power; Carthaginian ships travel to West Africa; Corsica, Sardinia, West Sicily, Malta, the Balearics and areas of Spain are conquered.

264–241: Beginning of the struggle between Rome and Carthage for the western Mediterranean; 1st Punic War; Carthage loses Sicily.

237: Corsica and Sardinia go over to Rome.

218–201: 2nd Punic War. The Carthaginian general Hannibal leaves Spain with 50,000 men and 60 elephants on his crossing of the Alps, and marches into Italy from the north. The Carthaginians are driven out of Spain.

149–146: 3rd Punic War. Destruction of Carthage, the territory of which becomes a Roman province.

1st c. A.D: Founding of Roman Carthage; large areas of North Africa are brought together to form the Roman province of Africa Proconsularis.

4th c: Christendom expands.

439–534: Rule by the Vandals who invade from Spain.

533: Belisarius destroys the Vandal kingdom; Tunisia becomes a province of the Byzantine Empire.

7th c: Invasion by the Arabs.

670: Founding of Kairouan, the first purely Arab town.

800–909: The Aghlabid Dynasty.

909–973: The Fatimid Dynasty; seat of government at Mahdia.

975–1159: The Zirid Dynasty.

1056: Invasion by the Berbers; destruction of a large part of the country.

1180: Beginning of the rule of the Almohads with Tunis as capital.

1228–1634: Hafsid Dynasty.

1535: Emperor Charles V conquers Tunis for Spain.

1574: Attack by the Turks; Tunisia becomes part of the Ottoman Empire.

About 1600: Great waves of Muslims and Jews return from Spain.

1705–1957: Husseinite Dynasty (Bey of Tunis).

1861: First Tunisian constitution.

1881: Tunisia becomes a French Protectorate.

1934: Habib Bourguiba founds the Neo-Destour party striving for independence.

1942/43: Battles on Tunisian soil between the Allies and the German Afrika Korps.

1956: Tunisia becomes independent.

1957: The Bey is deposed; Habib Bourguiba becomes first president.

1963: France withdraws from Biserta.

1964: Sequestration of foreign property.

1979: Tunis becomes the headquarters of the Arab League.

1981: First free elections.

1987: Zine El Abedine Ben Ali becomes the new president.

Phases of History

The following is a brief account of Tunisia's history. Only with a knowledge of the past in this age-old land of culture can you understand what the archaeological sites, the museums, the buildings and the works of art in Tunisia have to say.

The Carthaginians (9th–2nd c. B.C.)

The area now known as Tunisia bore the name of Africa centuries before the whole continent was so called. Way back in history it was inhabited by the Berbers, a rough but highly gifted, fair-skinned nomadic people of Hamitic origin who founded several independent kingdoms in North Africa.

At the end of the 13th c. B.C. Phoenician seafarers, voyaging from Asia Minor to Andalusia, landed at the Gulf of Tunis to set up several trading places, the first being *Utica*, today an interesting excavation site. Thus began the true history of Tunisia under the influence of the old Orient, even though its identity was not clearly defined at the time. It took shape with the founding of Carthage in the year 814 B.C.

The rich Phoenicians who inhabited the coast of Lebanon — a Semitic race — probably sailed to countries new in order to escape from the growing dominance of, and plundering by, the Assyrians. Legend has it otherwise — it says that the beautiful Princess Dido fled from the tyranny of her brother with her faithful followers to Utica, where a tribal chieftain promised them as much land 'as the hide of an ox will cover'. The clever princess cut the ox-hide into wafer-thin strips and laid claim to an area of land, on a peninsula, big enough to build a city. She named it *Kart-Hadascht*, meaning New City, which later became Carthage, the metropolis of a great empire. The commercial republic of Carthage quickly annexed all Phoenician settlements on African soil, sent its ships out into the Atlantic and in adventurous voyages established extremely profitable trading between East and West. However, when making constant attempts, initially thwarted by the Greeks, to set foot on nearby Sicily, it came into conflict with Rome. Thus began a struggle for power lasting a century and a half which, in three campaigns known as the Punic Wars, led to the fall of Carthage (named *Punis* by the Romans).

The untiring demand of the Roman Cato, who after each meeting of the Senate uttered the famous words 'I believe that Carthage must be destroyed,' was fully met; Carthage was razed to the ground in 146 B.C. The city, which is said to have had 700,000 inhabitants at the start of this final, three-year war, burned for seventeen days. Palaces, ships, places of worship were all laid low.

The Roman Province of Africa (2nd c. B.C.–5th c. A.D.)

The 'accursed soil of Carthage' was strewn with salt on the orders of the Roman Senate and was to remain undeveloped for all time. Yet a hundred years later Caesar, who assembled his army on the coast on his way to Egypt, planned to build a colony for veterans near the old city, and under Emperor Augustus a new (now Roman) Carthage came into being. As can be seen today from excavations everything, except some sacrificial altars and grave stelai, stems from Roman times, during which Tunisia became the well irrigated granary of Rome and a cultural centre of the ancient world.

Well preserved mosaics from this period, the most beautiful of which are owned by

Carthage

the Bardo Museum in Tunis (see page 35), portray the African variety of Greco-Roman living in both realistic and fantastic representations of hunting, banquets, harvesting and fishing. Punic and Roman gods became reconciled: the human sacrifices (condemned even in the ancient world) to the Carthaginian goddess *Tanit* (see page 38) were replaced by the sacrifice of animals and fruit to Caelestis, and *Baal Hammon* acquired the characteristics of Saturn and Jupiter.

At the same time spiritual and religious influences from the East grew. After the destruction of Jerusalem by Titus (A.D. 70) more and more followers of Yahveh migrated, and in spite of persecution by the Roman authorities the number of Christians increased, especially among the Berbers. Countless Christian martyrs stem from the African 'Province' and in the catacombs of Sousse rest the bones of 15,000 Christians who were buried there in the 2nd and 3rd centuries. Augustine, who was a Father of the Church and one of the greatest Christian thinkers, was a Berber from Tunisia. From Carthage Latin became the language of the Catholic Liturgy.

The Romans founded a great number of towns and cities and of course the most imposing of them remained Carthage which, towards the end of the 2nd c. A.D., was said to have had some 300,000 inhabitants once again. Other important places were the present-day Dougga, Teboursouk and Ain Tounga, which possessed notable buildings. To the most important towns the Romans laid on their water systems which still amaze us today; for instance, from the water source at Djebel Zaghouan ('Mons Ziquensis') 400 litres of water a second flowed over 124 km on aqueducts to Carthage.

Vandals and Byzantines (5th–7th c. A.D.)

The province in this epoch was certainly not free of social pressures accompanied by religious unrest. This uncertainty in the African provinces grew the more the Roman Empire in Europe fell under the onslaught of the German hordes. The most feared of them, the Vandals under Geiseric, came from Spain, landing in the year 439 at Cap Bon, and unhindered by the weak Roman occupation force took possession of Carthage. From here they set off in the year 455 on their successful plundering expedition to Rome!

The destructive reign of the Vandals was ended by the landing of a Byzantine army under Belisarius, who annexed the country for the Emperor Justinian. So in 533 Tunisia came under Byzantium and at once setting a defensive ring of powerfully fortified buildings, square forts with strong towers, was constructed along the coasts. In spite of this precaution Byzantine rule was short. It was the last epoch of Christian Tunisia and lasted scarcely more than a hundred and fifty years.

Its end was clearly indicated when Arab influence made itself felt. In 645–646 the Exarch Gregory was defeated in an attack under the leadership of Ibn Sarh. In 695 Carthage was destroyed by Hassan Ibn Noaman. Berber tribes under their leader Koceila and later under the heroic woman leader Kahena tried to put up resistance. After their defeat the Berber tribes went over to Islam. At the end of the 8th c. the Emirs of the Aghlabids made themselves independent of the rule of the Abbasids. Then came the great surge of the Arab-Mussulman conquerors from the land of the Caliph, who gave the territory the name of *Ifriquia*.

Arab Rule (8th–16th c. A.D.)

Christian Berbers and Byzantines fought together, but in vain, against the new enemy. Under the leadership of the Emir Okba Ben Nafi the fast horsemen penetrated deep into the interior. Near the spring where they rested their horses they founded in 670 the first purely Arab city on Tunisian soil, Kairouan, which was soon to become the seat of government, trading centre, fortress and Holy City of Islam in North Africa.

At the beginning of the 8th c. the Berbers were for the most part defeated, the Byzantines forced out of the country and Christian Africa was no more. In place of Carthage, which had been destroyed for the second time, the formerly unimportant *Tunes*, the Tunis of today, moved up to the rank of a city. History prevented the gradual evolution of a unified and progressive culture in Tunisia, for a succession of conquerors constantly changed everything completely. Only the Byzantine fortifications, for practical reasons, were taken over by the Arabs. They converted them into *ribats*, defensive castles, some of which are preserved to this day. The most impressive of these ribats are to be found in Sousse and Monastir. In accordance with their life-style the Arabs built no dwelling houses, only castles, palaces, guest houses *(fondouks)*, shopping bazaars *(souks)* and mosques, for the embellishment of which they used mainly pillars from Roman buildings.

The Caliphs of Baghdad assured themselves of political dominance by appointing Arab governors. With the governor Ibrahim Ibn al Aghlab, on whom was bestowed the hereditary title of Emir, began the famous dynasty of the Aghlabids, under whom the most important mosque-building work was carried out (A.D. 800–909). For example, the Great Mosque in Kairouan was completely renewed, and the Olive Tree Mosque

Ribat and mosque, Monastir

(Djamaa Ez-Zitouna) in Tunis (730, by Hassan Ibn Noaman) and the mosques of Sousse and Sfax (which was later altered) were constructed.

The Aghlabids were superseded by the Fatimids, who traced their origin back to Fatima, the daughter of Mohammed. The Fatimids conquered Egypt, founded the later city of Cairo and established their royal seat on the Nile. El Mahdi founded his capital Mahdia in the year 910. When unrest arose in Tunisia as a result of having to pay dues to the Fatimid kingdom, the ruler sent the nomadic tribes of Beni-Hilal on a punitive expedition into his homeland. That meant a second, extremely savage Arab invasion in which Tunisia was extensively laid to waste and Kairouan destroyed in 1057. It took the country a full hundred years to recover from the three-year 'Hilalic invasion' — a period of weakness, which was exploited to the full in attacks on its coastal towns by invaders from Genoa, Pisa and Normandy.

A fresh period of prosperity began again under the Almohads and Hafsids who reigned from the 12th to the 16th c. They were connected through trade and diplomacy with all the Christian courts and attracted many new, well educated and rich citizens into the country — merchants, doctors, academics and artisans. Most came from Spain, from where the Moors and Jews were being driven out. New quarters grew up in the towns, such as the 'Andalusian Quarter' in Biserta, and in the souks, the bazaars of Tunis, business flourished through the influx of skilled goldsmiths, dyers, perfumers, carpet weavers and dealers in cotton.

Under the Spaniards, Turks and French (16th–20th c.)

Its strategically important position close to Sicily dragged Tunisia once again into foreign power struggles, this time between the Spaniards and the Turks. In 1534 the bold corsair Khair Eddine, the notorious Barbarossa, seized Tunis and deposed the Hafsids. One year later Charles V annexed the area for the Spanish throne, mainly in order to deprive the pirates of their North African hiding-place. After 40 years of Spanish rule Tunis and La Goulette were reconquered in 1574 by the Turks, under the leadership of Sinan Pasha.

The resultant unstable power of the rulers encouraged many of the large ports to form their own city states, the principal income of which was derived from piracy. Next to the Algerian, the Tunisian pirate was the most feared on the high seas. The *raïs*, as the corsair leaders were called, seized numerous ships, took captive the Spaniards voyaging to America and drove long lines of prisoners to the great slave-market in Tunis. Piracy produced 'state income' by means of which many of the most important buildings, such as the Yussuf Bey Mosque in Tunis, were financed. More peaceful trading developed with the gradual reduction of the slave-trade in the 17th c. This also involved Genoese and French merchants, as well as a Jewish colony from Leghorn (Livorno), who opened offices in Tunisia.

The economic influence of France in the last century was increasingly followed by the political. Having heavily involved itself financially by supporting a Bey, France demonstrated its military strength by means of a surprise landing of its fleet in La Goulette. In 1881 Tunisia had to accept the status of a French Protectorate.

Thanks to modern reforms, the 75 years of the Protectorate produced a certain economic upswing, but one in which the mass of the people had only a small share. The increasing desire for independence led to the formation in 1934 of the Neo-Destour Party, committed to that cause and led by Habib Bourguiba. In the Second World War large parts of Tunisia were involved in the battles between the German Afrika Korps and the Allied Forces. While the damage in the towns has been mostly repaired, rusted cannon in the desert sands, dilapidated bunkers and large military cemeteries still remind us of the bitter struggle.

Not until 1956 was the fight for independence successful and finally, in 1963, the French relinquished the last town, the naval base of Biserta, to the young socialist republic. Habib Bourguiba, the elected father of the people since 1957, was forced because of his age to hand over to the new president, Ben Ali, in 1987.

🎨 For the Art lover

From the Carthaginian Period: The examples of Tunisian art reflect the art forms of the conquerors of the day. From the early period of the comparatively inartistic Carthaginians mainly votive statuettes and commemorative columns survive, including the very moving grave stelai for the children offered as sacrifices to Tanit. Small utensils such as oil lamps, perfume bottles and amphorae show little creative originality; the ability of this race of traders is best shown by the multiplicity of copper and gold coins.

   From the Roman Period: From the period of pagan Rome there are impressive remains of Roman-African towns (Carthage, Bulla Regia, Dougga, Thuburbo Majus, Maktar, Sbeitla, El Djem), as well as magnificent mosaics and a wealth of statues and statuettes, including contemporary imports from Greece.

El Djem

Islamic Art: Mosque architecture, which came with the Arabs, produced a powerful style in North Africa under the influence of the Berbers, giant square towers being typical. With the Turks came the domed buildings originally taken over from Byzantium, with slender round or octagonal minarets. Islamic art, which prohibits the representation of the living (which is why the old people are today still reluctant to be photographed), produced instead a vast multiplicity of artistically stylised ornaments, the 'pattern without end'. Small miracles of ornamental art are to be found in the ceramic tiles which frequently adorn walls as, for instance, in the 'Barber Mosque' in Kairouan.

Moorish elements: In Tunisia, as in the whole of North Africa, the special component of the Moorish style, influenced by the Spanish, is seen in the ornamentation as well as in the architecture. Delicate decorative elements come to the fore, breaking up the surfaces of the façades by means of grilles, columns and arches. As with many architectural forms, many of the Arabesque patterns have remained unchanged through the centuries. They celebrate their greatest triumph in the wonderful work of the stucco artists who carved beautiful fairytale shapes in the plaster ceilings of mosques and palaces.

Food and Drink

You can eat true Tunisian food in small restaurants everywhere, and 'true Tunisian' means lots of olive oil and very spicy flavours. Most native specialities can be found in a 'mild' form in restaurants which serve international cuisine. Do try:

Merguez: Appetisingly spiced sausage made from mutton or beef, cooked on a grill.

Mechoui: Grilled lamb.

Mirmiz: Mutton braised with beans, tomatoes and potatoes.

Objabilmerguez: Sausage in a spicy tomato sauce with potatoes, lots of garlic and eggs.

Salade Michouia: A spicy salad made from tomato and paprika purée with onions, capers, tuna fish, eggs and olive oil.

Couscous: This most famous North African dish is not to be found every day even in the best places! A tradition-conscious cook prepares couscous on Friday, the Islamic Sabbath. Couscous is coarse semolina, or millet can be used instead. In a complicated preparation process the semolina is simmered in a special finely perforated couscous pot until it swells. The softened couscous is richly garnished. Usually you will be asked whether you would like your couscous with mutton, chicken or fish. A lot of vegetables will be heaped on it and then the whole mountain of couscous will have a well spiced, fatty stock poured over it. If it should by any chance not be hot enough for your taste you can always add more spice. In addition to salt and pepper you will be passed the special Tunisian spice *harissa*. If you put a pinch of this on your tongue your eyes will flood with tears! Harissa is made from dried, crushed, salted and oiled peppercorns and a little tomato purée.

For dessert the Tunisians like things much sweeter:

Makrud: Pastry or semolina slices covered with crushed dates, baked in oil and then dipped in honey.

Baklaua: Puff pastry, often filled with date or fig jam, cooked in oil and with sugar- or honey-water poured over it.

Bjaouia: A cake filled with a mixture of almonds, pistachio nuts and puffed rice.

Beach party

Brik (for 4 persons)

125 gr. minced meat (preferably mixed lamb and beef), 1 large onion, 3 cloves of garlic, 1 sprig of parsley, butter, salt, pepper, paprika (hot), flour, 4 eggs, vegetable oil.

First knead a 'malsuka' dough from 200 gr. coarse flour, 1 cup of water and a pinch of salt, and leave in the warm for 15 minutes.

Meanwhile mix the minced meat with the finely chopped onion, garlic and parsley, add salt and season with pepper and paprika. Simmer in butter until all the liquid has disappeared. Then roll out the dough quite thinly on a floured surface, cut out 4 squares of approx. 25x25 cm, pile the filling into the centre of each square and break an egg on it. Fold the dough diagonally into a triangle, firm the edges and deep fry the *Brik* in hot vegetable oil (or shallow fry in a pan).

Wines, Spirits and Fruit Juices

Wines from Tunisia have been famous for their excellent quality for over 2000 years. Even the ancient Carthaginians ran a profitable trade around the Mediterranean with their grape juices. Tunisian certified wines are strictly controlled by the state; they may not be 'refined' and must come solely from the area of cultivation shown on the bottle.

Red wines are heavy and fruity. They include *Sidi Saad* (in a graceful amphora bottle), *Magon* (the name recalls a relative of Hannibal who edited the first written instructions on wine production), *Château Feriani, Lamblot* and *Vieux Thibar*.

Rosé wines are ideal with food. A few names are *Château Mornag, Haut Mornag, Gris de Tunisie, Hidalgo, Thibar, Koudiat, Domaine Karim, Rosé Muscat de Dougga* and *Sidi Rais*.

White wines in Tunisia are fruity and dry. *Muscat de Kilibia* is the star among them; also not to be despised is the white *Sidi Rais*.

High proof: A well known liqueur called *Thibarine* is produced in the Thibar district. *Boukha* is made from first-class figs. This fig brandy forms the basis of many apéritifs and also a 'booster' for coke or coffee.

Beer: The three brands of Tunisian beer are *Celtia, 33 de Luxe* and *Stella*. They are all perfectly drinkable.

Low-alcohol and alcohol-free: A very slightly alcoholic drink, *Lagmi*, will be offered to you at the date oases. This date brandy is not obtained from the fruit but runs like resin or rubber from an incision in the trunk. Older Lagmi really tests the digestion. You can, of course, also live without alcohol in Tunisia. There are several types of mineral water, including *Melitti, Ain Garci, Ain Oktar* or *Safia*. Fruit juices can be bought fresh or bottled according to the season. A sweet milky drink called *orgeat* is pressed from almonds. Fruit syrups of all kinds are served with Tunisian lemonade, *boga*.

Coffee and tea can be obtained at any time of the day. In Turkish coffee (*café à la turque*) a few drops of rose water are added. If you ask for Tunisian tea you will receive a thick, over-sweet brew enriched with peppermint. The Tunisian *thé à la menthe*, however, is very different from that in neighbouring North African countries.

Shopping

It is fun to stroll through the souks, the bazaar streets of the old town. However, bazaar prices are not necessarily better than those in the art and craft shops with the word 'Artisanat' over the window. Here you will find a variety of Tunisian craftwork on sale — ceramics, copper articles, wood carvings, camel-leather goods, wrought iron, lace, jewellery, toys and, in particular, dolls in traditional dress.

Jewellery: traditional Bedouin jewellery, triangular or square silver shields, smooth armbands of heavy silver, brooches set with colourful stones and jangling chains of many kinds can all cause a sensation at home as fashion jewellery. New objects are often primitively mass produced, while the old and somewhat worn are more expensive but much nicer. In the south the choice is far greater.

Carpets: well worth considering is the purchase of hand-woven or knotted Tunisian carpets (*tapis*) or hangings, which well established firms will send home for you. Kairouan carpets are renowned far and wide. The quality depends on the number of knots per square metre. The different qualities are as follows:-

Qualité supérieure (best quality with more than 90,000 knots per square metre),

Premier choix (over 40,000 knots), and

Deuxième choix (over 12,000 knots).

If you buy a carpet you should make sure that it is marked with the official quality mark of the *Office Nationale de l'Artisanat Tunisien* (ONAT).

The carpets are mostly named after the region or place where they are made and have their own typical patterns and colours. The *Biserta*, for example, is reddish-brown or violet and has a large central field surrounded by stripes. The *Kairouan* is white, black and beige; the central field often displays a lozenge-shaped medallion in red, framed by five to eight borders. Very similar to the Kairouan is the *Sahel*. The *Khroumiri* has a beige or brown background and a geometric pattern.

The best-known woven wall-hangings, the *kelims*, include those of *Gafsa* with their square fields on which can be seen stylised men, animals and palms, and the carpets of *Gabès* with colourful figure motifs on a single-colour background.

 Festivals and events

On the island of Djerba foreigners are shown all kinds of wedding traditions in the form of colourful public festivals, and in various Roman theatres performances of classical dramas are given during the season. However, the most beautiful and interesting festivals, which have evolved from the lives of the people and go far beyond mere tourist entertainment, are the religious ones celebrated by the Muslims and Jews. Thus, for example, we have the great feast of *Aid Esseghir* which marks the end of the fasting month of Ramadan, when the streets are filled with children. They proudly wear their new clothes, bought especially for this day, and make a deafening noise with flutes, horns and pipes. Also celebrated are *El Mouled*, the birthday of the

Prophet, and the Feast of the Ram, *L'Aid el Kebir*, which commemorates the sacrifice of Isaac who is represented by a ram. For days beforehand the children walk the beribboned sheep, the flesh of which is subsequently distributed to the poor.

The Jewish feast of *Yom Kippur*, the Feast of Forgiveness, is celebrated in a very lively and colourful fashion in autumn in the Jewish villages on Djerba. Especially rich in colourful scenes is the *Ghriba* festival in May, to which come Jewish pilgrims from all parts of the Orient.

Muslim feast days are fixed in accordance with the moon calendar and as the moon-year is shorter than the sun-year, they move further forward in our calendar each year.

State festivals are: January 1st; Independence Day, March 20th; Youth Day, March 21st; Day of the Martyrs, April 9th; Labour Day, May 1st; Republic Day, June 25th; Women's Day, August 13th.

The most important of the many popular festivals of only local importance are mentioned in the descriptions of the places concerned.

H Moorish steam baths

A healthy Tunisian pleasure can be experienced in the *hammam* and a hammam can be found almost everywhere. The ideal hammam draws its water from a thermal spring, as in Hammam-Lif, in Korbous or in Djebel Oust near Zaghouan, to name only a few. Others use simple tap-water heated to bath temperature.

In addition to sweating and bathing, the body is worked on by an attendant with rough linen cloths, and in the best hammams legs and arms are also put through the mill, twisted, pulled and bent until you do not know which toe belongs to which foot. But afterwards you feel a new man — or woman.

There are, of course, no 'unisex hammams'. Most hammams are open to both sexes, but at different times!

Sports and games

Most hotels offer plenty in the way of facilities for sports and games, mostly free for hotel guests. You need not be afraid to enquire at a neighbouring hotel if they have a facility which your hotel cannot offer. Here and there you may come across private concerns which hire motor boats, but it is doubtful if their craft are comprehensively insured so nobody would accept liability for accidents.

On the beaches or in the nearby harbours you will be certain to find fishermen who will take you out on a trip with them — often they will approach you and offer their services or, if not, the hotel will arrange a boat for you. Everywhere, too, you will be offered rides on asses, camels and horses, which carry happy-looking tourists along the beach with measured stride. However gentle-looking the horses, they should only be trusted (unless they are old ones!) if you have some riding experience. An unexpected break into a gallop can quickly bring a pleasant ride to an abrupt end.

The surfaces of the hotel tennis courts are not always up to European standards and there are not many public courts. Golf courses exist in Tunis, in Port El Kantaoui and in Monastir. Land-surfing is one of the attractions of the country, and this sport can be tried out on the salt-flats of Chott El Djerid near Tozeur.

Hints for your holiday

'When in Tunisia...'

Tunisia is an Islamic country and moral concepts are different from those in Europe, even if this is not obvious at first sight.

For a Muslim the consumption of alcohol is a sin, even though many Tunisians do drink wine and beer. The serving of alcoholic drinks is prohibited before 12 noon; after 8 p.m. it is allowed only in 'International' restaurants and hotel bars. The rule was made for the benefit of European tourists, but Tunisians can also benefit.

Another problem arises in relation to women. Islam is a masculine religion which determines social structures and values accordingly. Even the reforms of the former State President Bourguiba did not alter that to any degree. Apart from in Tunis, Sfax and Sousse, it is demanded of women that they behave and dress in accordance with the rules of Islam. Bikinis are, therefore, tolerated on the beaches of the large hotels but not when strolling through villages.

You should behave as unobtrusively as possible when visiting mosques, and they may only be entered if you are 'completely' dressed. For men that means long trousers, and for women, being very well covered. Shoes must be removed at the entrance to the mosque. It is thus useful to have socks with you.

With a few words of Arabic you can readily strike up a trusting relationship with the more simple people. The Tunisian is delighted if you ask after his family, but you should not enquire directly regarding his wife. Also it is a breach of good manners to speak to a woman in the street. However, the Tunisians themselves do not stick to this rule where European ladies are concerned.

Should you be invited into a Tunisian family, accept the invitation gracefully and you will find the whole family in a state of frantic upheaval. A European guest is both an honour and an obligation. If, instead of a bunch of flowers, you take with you a box of small cakes and tarts, you will be regarded as a perfectly mannered gentleman. Do not be surprised if, having accepted your gift, the master of the house then puts it in a corner apparently without paying it much attention. That is in fact good manners. You can rest assured that as soon as you have left the house the whole family will descend upon the sweetmeats.

It is also good manners to use only the right hand while eating; the left is regarded as unclean.

Where to go and what to see

The North

The north is the region with the most abundant supply of water, the most fertile and economically the most advanced. The Atlas Mountains, rising to heights of four thousand metres in Morocco, gradually become lost here in a hilly landscape, the highest point of which is the 1544-m-high Djebel Chambi. Its final foothills form the steep peak of Cap Bon.

The North Tunisian countryside is romantic in so many ways; cork-oak forests, the last home for Atlas deer and eagles, and small reservoirs are to be found in the western corner near the Algerian border. In the north-east the 30-km-wide peninsula of Cap Bon, extending like a long finger far into the Mediterranean, forms one of the most delightful pieces of landscape in North Africa and is particularly rich in plant life.

On your travels in the north of Tunisia you will come across sights and colours similar to those in southern Europe: walls covered in bougainvillea, gardens with grapes, apricots and pomegranates, fields of tomatoes and orange-groves.

Countryside and history together offer sights well worth seeing; in the north much is preserved which tells of the history of European occupation of this African country. Quite unexpectedly Roman triumphal arches of the past rise from the landscape of today; the capitals of Corinthian columns are outlined against the still, blue African sky; amphitheatres, temples and water-tanks standing desolate remind us of times when the power of the Roman Empire was at its height.

Tourism in the north is concentrated on the coast which stretches from the coral town of Tabarka in the extreme north-west, via Biserta and Tunis, to the famous holiday centres of the country, Nabeul and Hammamet, in the east. The Gulf of Hammamet is cosmopolitan Africa, a mixture of holiday paradise and gold-mining boom, a giant playground of carefree holiday mood, encircled by an impressive panorama patterned with lush gardens and edged with flat sandy beaches stretching for miles.

Tunis Pop. 800,000 in the city zone, 1.7 million in the whole conurbation. Tunis, 'The Green City' — *Tunes El Ehadra* — is said to be becoming more modern and at the same time more beautiful and more pleasant to live in! And that is being done mainly with Arab oil billions. People are investing in Tunis, just as they are everywhere else in Tunisia. For some years Tunis has been the headquarters of the Arab League, not only an Arab banking centre but also an international one, a university city and, not least, the administrative centre of Tunisia. All in all Tunis is the only really major city in the country.

At present Tunis is full of building sites, and it will certainly remain so for some years. The German firm of Siemens AG

is building an urban and suburban railway, the canal system is being extended and re-sited, fast roads are appearing and a motorway bypassing the city is already more than half finished. You can already drive to Hammamet on it and it is planned to extend it as far as Sousse.

Tunis lies at the end of a lagoon, 50 sq. km in area, shallow and full of fish, called the *Lac de Tunis*, in Arabic *El Bahira* — 'the small sea'. Parts of the lake are at present being filled in, to provide building ground for a new city quarter and an international exhibition centre. A 10-km-long dam, constructed at the end of the 19th c., over which run the suburban line and the motorway, divides the lake and connects Tunis with the open sea and the deep-water harbour of La Goulette. Near the dam a canal runs through the lagoon, enabling the larger ships to put into the city harbour of Tunis.

The lagoon also offers other attractions; the shallow water is an ideal hunting ground for sea-birds seeking fish and crabs. Flocks of pink flamingos pick at crabs. The small island with its ruins of a Turkish castle has been declared a protected bird-sanctuary. Numerous types of waterfowl breed here. Tunis is surrounded by salt lakes which dry out in summer, when their layers of salt glisten like ice rinks. They fill up after the first autumn rains and flocks of flamingos and herons arrive.

A chain of hills borders the Gulf of Tunis in the south. The mountain with two peaks is the 576-m-high *Djebel Bou Kornine* (The Mountain of Two Horns).

🐚 History

Tunis, *Tunes* in the ancient world, one of the oldest settlements on the Mediterranean, first became an important town with the invasion of the Arabs. When the Arabs ruled Tunisia and Sicily, they moved their seat of government, first of all for a short period in the 9th c., from the city of Kairouan in the interior to the protected Bay of Tunis. It quickly developed into a trading town and finally became the capital under the Almohads in the 12th c. Its period of greatest prosperity was under the Hafsids (13th–16th c.). It surpassed Cairo and its wealth was mentioned in the same breath as that of the Caliph city of Baghdad.

After an unsuccessful siege by the Crusaders under Louis the Holy (1270), Tunis committed itself to granting to the Christians living within its walls freedom of belief, trade, and the building of churches, a form of tolerance which it later also displayed towards its Jewish inhabitants. After a short period of Spanish rule the Turks conquered the city in 1574 and remained official rulers until 1920. In fact, of course, the Bey of

Tunis had renounced them as long ago as 1705. In 1881 Tunis became the seat of the French Résident-Général for the Protectorate, and during the last war it was occupied by the Germans for a year. In 1956 it became the capital and seat of government of the independent Republic of Tunisia.

📷 A walk round the city

The present-day city consists of two very different parts. Typically oriental in character is the Old Town, the Medína (emphasis on the second syllable), which was named the 'Hooded Cloak of the Prophet' by imaginative chroniclers, because of its white houses on the hills above. On the other hand, the New Town, which grew up during the period of the protectorate and is laid out with the regularity of a chessboard, could be any average-sized French town.

Do not be afraid to hail one of the numerous taxis driving past; for 3 dinars it will take you through the whole of Tunis.

The New Town. Easy to find: drive straight along the *Avenue Habib Bourguiba* and its extension the *Avenue de France* for 1.5 km from the harbour as far as the gate to the Medina. Planted with four rows of plane and palm trees, the Avenue Habib Bourguiba looks like a Tunisian variation of the Champs Elysées. At the large kiosks on this avenue, you can find British newspapers and periodicals. Papers and magazines appear mostly in Arabic and French. The most important daily papers in French are *La Presse, Le Temps* and the party newspaper *L'Action*.

In its western section Avenue Habib Bourguiba is crossed by an equally long main road, which in its southerly direction is called Avenue de Carthage (the arterial road to Hammamet and Sousse), and in its northerly direction

Right: Tunis

first Avenue de Paris and then Avenue de la Liberté.

Where the two avenues cross you will find popular meeting places, such as the Café de Paris. Here you can sit undisturbed and study the great variety of the Tunisian populace — Arabs, Berbers, Europeans, fair- and dark-skinned faces — in a constantly changing picture. Scarcely any of the Tunisian women in Tunis itself still wear the typical *sefsari*, the nun-like white dress in expensive damask, mostly held

in place with the teeth. The men are dressed in European clothes and only on hot summer days will you sometimes see them in the cool *djebba*, a white embroidered robe without arms, reaching down to the calves.

West from the crossing, in the direction of the Medina, on the left side of the Avenue Habib Bourguiba, stands the state art and crafts centre, the *Maison de l'Artisanat*, ONAT. Here, without obligation, you can obtain information about the prices of carpets, ceramics,

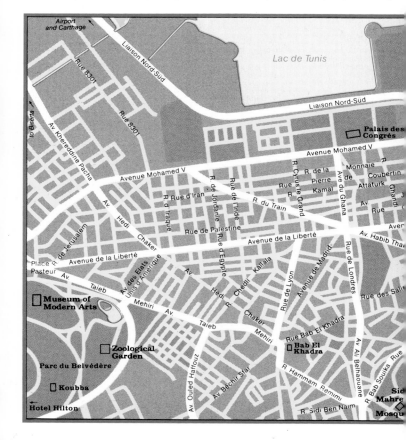

traditional clothing and jewellery — no compulsion to purchase, but there is a 10% loading on the price if you pay in foreign currency. On the same side is the grandiose `art nouveau *Municipal Theatre*, and on the right side the *Cathedral*, built in the ostentatious French Colonial style of the last century. In front of the cathedral can be seen the statue of the city's most famous son, the historian, scientist and philosopher Ibn Khaldoun (1332–1406).

Going in an easterly direction along Avenue Habib Bourguiba (in the direction of the sea), you will pass the Africa-Meridian Hotel, which is clearly visible from afar, and then come to the *Place d'Afrique* with the statue of Habib Bourguiba on horseback. Here you will find the information bureau, the *Office de Tourisme*.

Some 300 m past the Place d'Afrique on the right are the termini of the Métro Léger, which goes via the main railway station to the southern suburbs, and the TGM, the Tunis-Goulette-Mares

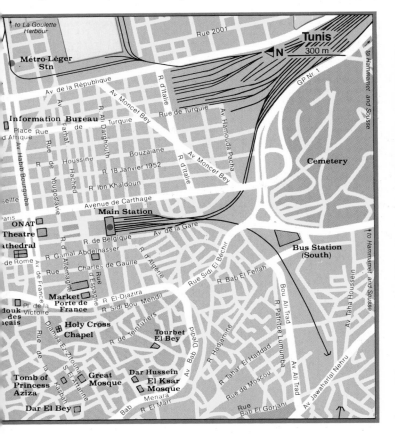

Highly decorated architecture

suburban railway; trains run every 10 minutes between 5 a.m. and 8.30 p.m. to the suburbs in the direction of Carthage. When passing over the 10-km dam section the train stops about every kilometre.

Belvédère. At the Place d'Afrique begins Avenue Mohammed V, which leads to the elegant quarter of Belvédère, home of the Embassy buildings and smart villas. Avenue Mohammed V ends at the municipal park of Tunis, the *Parc du Belvédère*. Here are an open-air swimming pool, a magnificently laid out zoological garden (established with the help of the city of Cologne which is twinned with Tunis), and finally, on the slopes of the 82-m-high Belvédère Hill, a charming small pavilion, the *Koubba*, an 18th c. building decorated in exquisite stucco work. From here a further panorama beckons. Near the Koubba in the former casino is housed the Museum of Modern Arts *(Centre d'art vivant du Belvédère)*. On summer evenings concerts are held in the park-like museum gardens. If you walk through the Parc du Belvédère you will reach in about 15 minutes the towering Tunis Hilton hotel, a good landmark. Passing the Hilton you will meet the Voie X, the bypass which connects the Bardo area of the town with the airport and the northern coastal suburbs. On the far side of the road lie the University campus and the modern quarter of El Menzah. Today Tunis is also a convention and exhibition centre. Near the Place d'Afrique on Avenue Mohammed V is the shell-shaped *Palais des Congrès* with mainly international exhibitions; at the beginning of Avenue de Carthage we find the municipal *Galerie Yahia* and near the cathedral in Avenue Habib Bourguiba are the *Exhibition Rooms of the Ministry of Information*. The Third World, especially the Arab and African states, likes to rendezvous in Tunis.

The Medina. Buses drive round it and you can get off at any convenient stopping place. However, in the old town itself there is no traffic at all. That means you have to walk through the narrow, bumpy alleyways.

The *Porte de France* (Bab el Bhar, or Gateway to the Sea), at one time an entrance gate in the long-since demolished city wall, can be found at the end of Avenue de France. Near this gate was the earliest European settlement, the *Fondouk des Français*, the refuge of the French, the first district occupied by French merchants.

From the Porte de France the Rue Djamaa Ez-Zitouna, in which stands the Chapel of the *Holy Cross*, leads to the Great Mosque, the *Djamaa Ez-Zitouna* (Mosque of the Olive Tree), the courtyard and colonnade of which can be visited (8–11 a.m. daily except Friday). The building, erected in its present form in the 9th—15th c. and more recently renovated, contains beautiful ancient columns and Venetian chandeliers in the prayer hall where the sunlight plays through the windows.

This area is where the real *souks* begin, those alleyways of shops covered with high domes, which remain to this day in their traditional form. In the streets of the souks, however, you will find not only shops but also restaurants and coffee houses where you can drink Turkish coffee and also smoke a hubble-bubble pipe.

As in olden times, the individual streets are still arranged according to the trades to be found in them, and named after them. Sweet scents pervade the *Souk El Atterine* (Souk des Parfumeurs) with its shops often only as big as cupboards, in which you can have your own personal perfume mixed for you. It is worth noting that status-conscious traders will not serve you after lunch because after a good meal the sense of smell is impaired. The noise of loud hammering leads you to the

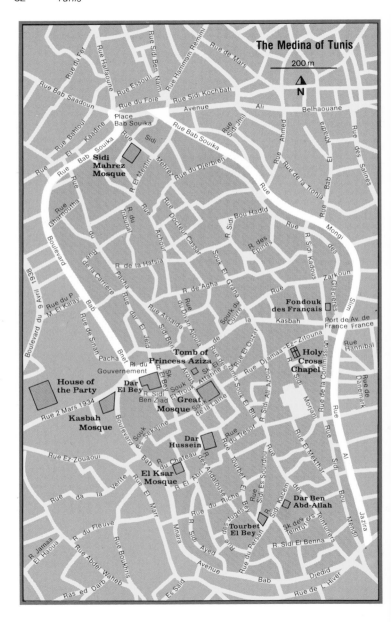

The Medina of Tunis

200 m

N

Rue du Fer
Rue Sidi Ben Naim
Rue Hammam Remini
Rue de Mars
Rue Hallaoune
Rue Essouli
Rue du Foie
Rue Sidi Kochbati
Rue Bab Saadoun
Avenue
Ali
Belhaouane
Place Bab Souika
Rue du Jmil
Rue Ahmed
Rue Battou
Rue Bab Souika
Rue El
Kaadine
Rue Bab Souika
Rue Sidi
Rue El
Sidi
Rue des Salines
Rue Bab Mestiri
Sidi Mahrez Mosque
R. El Mestiri
Rue du Djerbien
Rue de la Tronja
Rue Bab
R. du
Rue
Ghamoutha
Tribunal
R. Achour
Rue Docteur Cassar
R. Sidi Bou Hadid
Rue
Mongi
Boulevard
gend
R. de la Hafsia
Souk-El-Grana
R. des Epines
R. Sidi Kadous
Zarkoun
des
Rue de la Carrière
Pacha Rue dar El Jeld
R. de Agha
Souk du Cuivre
la
Rue
Slim
du 9 Avril 1938
Rue du P.
M. El Kalay
Bab
Rue Assalda
Rue du Divan Aloula
Fondouk des Français
Port de Av. de
Rue de Sinan
Sidi Ben
Kasbah
France France
Rue Hannibal
Pacha
Pl. du
Gouvernement
Tomb of Princess Aziza
Rue El Ourat
Rue Djamaa-Ez-Zitouna
Holy Cross Chapel
Rue de Danemark
House of the Party
Dar El Bey
Sidi Ben Ziad
Souk Attarine
Souk El Bac
Rue Sidi Ali Azour
Rue Sidi
Moriem
Rue de la Commission
Rue 2 Mars 1934
Souk
El Trouk
Great Mosque
Souk de la Laine
Kasbah Mosque
Boulevard
Souk es Sekkajine
Dar Hussein
Rue du Trésor
Rue El Mekthar
Rue Ez-Zouaoui
Bab
R. du Château
El Ksar Mosque
R. El Abir
Rue des Andalousie
Rue Touibet El Bey
Rue Es-Sourdou
Ali
Bou Mendri
Rue
da
la
Vente
Rue El Marr
Rue du Riche
Dar Ben Abd-Allah
R. Jamaa El Haoua
R. du Fleuve
Rue Abdel Waheb
Rue Boukhris
Mnara
Rue du Jubes
Rue Sidi Ayed
Tourbet El Bey
R. Kaceim
Sk. des Teinturiers
Jazira
Ras ed Darb
Avenue
Es Süd
Rue du Persan
R. Sidi El Benna
Bab
Djedid
Rue de l' Hiver

Copper souvenirs

coppersmiths who, for a small payment, will punch any name you require on your copper or brass souvenir bowls. When you come to the *Souk El Leffa*, go into the carpet shop called *Palais d'Orient*, belonging to Chadli et Othman Ben Ghorbal. Through this shop a staircase leads to a large terrace which is adorned with ceramic tiles of all ages, and presents a splendid sight.

After visiting the Great Mosque you should not finish your tour too soon:

South of the mosque you will enter a quarter of noble houses with Andalusian-Arab railings and beautiful ornaments, as well as the mausoleum of *Tourbet El Bey*, a green-domed 18th c. building decorated with rectangular windows, pilasters and cornices in the Italian style. All Beys who have died since 1782 lie in state here in accordance with their personal standing. On payment of a tip you will be able to visit the burial halls.

Nearby, in Rue Ben Abd-Allah, you can enter the exquisite palace of *Dar Abd-Allah*, which contains a museum of popular art and customs.

South-west of the Great Mosque you come to the *Souk des Orfèvres*, the labyrinth of silver- and goldsmiths, and via the *Souk El Leffa* (the Souk of Carpets) to the *Souk El Berka* and to a small square which is still reminiscent of the former slave market. After Algiers it was the second largest slave market in Africa. Further south we find the *Dar Hussein*, a 17th c. palace housing the National Institute of Archaeology and Art. Nearby stands the *El Ksar* Mosque (12th c.); the minaret displays the Spanish-Moorish style of the 17th c.

North-west of the Great Mosque between the Souk of the Slippermakers and that of the Perfumers lies the monument to Princess Aziza Othmana (ask for the *Tombe de la Princesse Aziza Othmana*); you will be shown into the entrancing courtyard of a private house. Its occupants will show you memorabilia of the Bey's daughter who died in 1646 and on whom, because of her kindness and good deeds, the people bestowed the epithet 'Aziza', meaning 'Beloved One'.

Via the Rue de la Kasbah you come to the Place du Gouvernement. On the left is the *Dar El Bey*, today the seat of the Prime Minister and the Foreign Minister. On the right are the Ministry of Trade and Commerce and the Ministry of Finance, with Arabic signs of the Zodiac on the clock tower.

At the upper end of the small square the bypass road leads past the Medina. On the opposite side of the road on the left stands the Ministry of Defence, at the corner of which rises the *Kasbah Mosque*, built in 1235, with its beautiful square minaret, the shape and stone ornamentation of which are reminiscent of the famous Kutubiah of Marrakesh. With luck — and a tip — you will be allowed to climb up the minaret.

Carry on in the same direction, along the asphalt road up Kasbah Hill (a huge car park is on the right), and you will pass

In the souks, Tunis

the Ministry of Culture on the left. On the right, the modern building with the round arches is the *House of the Party*, the headquarters of the governing party 'Rassemblement Constitutionnel Démocratique' (RCD). On the left the historic castle of Tunis is being rebuilt, having been demolished for house building. You come now to a second bypass road, the Avenue du 9 Avril. Here is the old Tunis University Building. If you stop just to the left you will have an extensive view of the salt lake of *Sedjoumi*. In the distance, far beyond the salt lake, you can see the geometric outlines of the 1295-m-high *Djebel Zaghouan* (some 60 km distant), from which the Romans piped their drinking water over an aqueduct to Carthage. Remains of this water-system can still be seen in Tunis itself and on the road to Zaghouan.

The Northern Medina. Passing through the Souk of the Slippermakers and past that of the sheet-metal workers, copper- and tinsmiths, you arrive at the *Place Bab Souika* (Gate to the Small Market). Here is the traditional centre of Tunis, a

quarter where tourists are seldom seen. The surrounding cafés set out their tables and chairs under a few evergreen trees. Here you can sit and rest at peace with the world. Alexandre Dumas describes it in his book on Tunisia and relates how a petty thief, having been sentenced to death by the Bey, would be set back to front on a donkey and driven to the Bab Souika amid the applause of the crowd, there to be put on show at the gate. Having placed a noose around his neck, the hangman would then push him off the gate. Today this spot has become a favourite meeting place during the wild nights of the Ramadan month of fasting.

The street leading away from the Place Bab Souika, which has been dedicated to Sidi Mahrez, the patron saint of the city, has a character quite different from most Medina streets; it seems more colourful, happier and rather more elegant. In this street, too, is the *Sidi Mahrez* Mosque (1675), which unlike the typical North African mosque with its heavy, angular minaret, has the elegance of the Turkish style which was borrowed from Constantinople.

At the weekend it becomes quieter in the Medina; on Fridays everything in the Rue Djamaa Ez-Zitouna is shut and on Sundays all the other souks are closed.

🐾 The Bardo Museum

The Alaoui National Museum in the suburb of Bardo, usually called simply *Musée de Bardo*, contains one of the most fascinating historical collections and is the most important archaeological museum in the Maghreb. The path through the well kept park to the former residence of the Turkish Bey is a delight.

The massive fortress-tower which borders the extensive palace gardens was once the barracks of the Bey's soldiers and was built in the 15th c.

At about the same time the first royal castles were erected. Over the centuries these buildings have been fitted out more and more luxuriously, especially during the period 1831 to 1855.

A great deal was spent on the sumptuous furnishings of the harem, the 'House of Women', with its numerous magnificent halls and discreet chambers. The splendour of the grandiose reign of the Turkish Bey came to a close at the end of the last century, when the 'Treaty of Bardo' (1881) made France the 'Protector' of the country.

Today, in the relatively small state rooms, watched over by smart guardsmen and two marble lions, sits the Tunisian parliament (Chambre des Députés). The museum is situated in the former harem. Only the old fortress-tower and the buildings attached still serve their original purpose. They provide accommodation for the soldiers who guard the Houses of Parliament.

You should plan a visit to the Bardo Museum for the first day of your stay in Tunisia. It will prepare you well for trips to the ancient places of cultural interest. The most valuable finds from historical

Fishing — Roman mosaic in the Bardo Museum

settlements are to be seen here. One further tip: the museum is less crowded just after it opens in the morning.

Art treasures of rare beauty and importance are displayed in over 40 rooms. Unique in its richness is the collection of mosaics in the Roman department. The mosaic of *Odysseus and the Sirens* has been on loan almost everywhere in the world. Equally worth seeing is the room — kept locked — containing jewellery and works in gold from Punic times. If the attendants are not too busy they will open it up on request.

Most impressive is the small Greek Department in the Mahdia Room. These examples of Hellenic art were taken as booty from Greece by the Romans in about 100 B.C., and brought to Africa; they went down with the ship off the coast near the present town of Mahdia, and were discovered by diving fishermen in 1907.

The Arab-Islamic Department is certainly worth a visit. The building is as luxurious as its contents. It was once a

By the Bardo Museum, Tunis

small palace of the Beys and is older than the main building attached to it in 1831.

For a fee, photographs can be taken in the museum, but without the use of a tripod or flash. Pretty souvenirs which can be purchased in the museum are theatrical masks in plaster, oil lamps, amulets and statuettes. (Opening times: daily 9.30 a.m.—4.30 p.m., except Mondays and official feast days.)

 The bathing-beaches of Tunis lie about 15 km outside the city. Most can be easily reached by the suburban railway TGM. However, swimming there is not very satisfactory from the point of view of hygiene, especially in the high season. Some of the yellow city buses go to the more remote beaches of Raouad (28 km) in summer.

 At *Gammarth-Plage, Amilcar-Carthage* and the other large hotels.

 Privately in La Goulette, yacht clubs in Sidi Bou Said, *Gammarth-Plage, Amilcar-Carthage*.

 At the harbour entrance of La Goulette.

 Piscine Municipale (municipal swimming pool) in Belvédère Park; Olympic stadium *Stadium Habib Bourguiba*, but this is often in use by swimming clubs. On payment of admission fee the swimming pools of the Hotels *Hilton* and *Africa*.

There are saunas everywhere in Tunisia. Ask for a hammam. However, they are separate for men and women, as regards both place and time. Your hotel porter can tell you where to find the nearest one.

On the beaches. *La Soukra* riding club (on the other side of the airport).

At La Soukra, on the far side of the airport; tel. 20 30 25.

Tunis Tennis Club, Av. Alain Savary (Belvédère).

The *Festival de Carthage* takes place in the summer months. In the ancient theatres of Carthage and Dougga theatre groups from all over the world perform ancient and modern plays, and musical events are also on the programme. French and Italian operas are performed in the Tunis Municipal Theatre. Well worth seeing are the horse races on the 'Kassar Said' (military riding school) course and the horse auctions, *Journée de l'Elevage*, in the first half of April at the stud farm about 20 km away in Sidi Thabet. Horse-lovers should not miss this on any account.

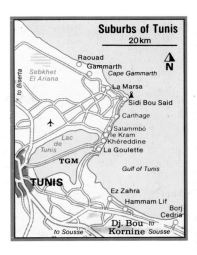

Oriental dances in *Le Malouf*, 108 Rue de Yougoslavie; in *Le M'rabet*, Souk Et-Trouk (Medina); also in the restaurants of the large hotels.

In the large hotels. The discothèques in the town are mostly very short-lived. Generally only for couples; individuals are often turned away.

Tunis Club, corner of Av. Habib Bourguiba and Av. de Paris; *Club 2001* in the *El Mechtel* and in most large hotels.

Arab-Tunisian cuisine: *Le Malouf*, 108 Rue de Yougoslavie; *Le Palais*, 6 Av. de Carthage; *Le M'rabet*, Souk Et-Trouk (Medina). Fish specialities in the city centre: *Le Regent*, Rue Azis Tej; *Le Carthage* and *L'Orient*, Rue Nahas Pascha; *Gaston*, Rue de Yougoslavie. Kosher food can be eaten in *Le Robinson*, Av. de Madrid.

French cuisine: many restaurants in the side streets off Av. Habib Bourguiba, e.g. *Strasbourg*, 100 Rue de Yougoslavie; *Chez Nous*, 5 Rue de Marseille; *La Rôtisserie* in the Hotel Africa. Dishes of the day are inexpensive.

Suburbs north of Tunis

La Goulette Pop. 42,000

Anyone who travels by sea first sets foot on Tunisian soil at La Goulette. This has been true since the 17th c. as the Tunis lagoon silted up more and more.

The much besieged town, fortified by the Spaniards and Turks as an important naval base, has a large trans-shipment harbour and is the home of a considerable fishing fleet.

From the *Fortress of La Karraka*, built by the Spaniards and extended by the Turks after 1574, there is an extensive view over the Gulf of Tunis and of the lively activity in the harbour quarter of La Goulette. In this fortress which for a long time served as a prison — the grim rooms are still to be seen — a folk-music and theatre festival takes place in summer.

 Bathing is not recommended on La Goulette beach.

 By the breakwater at the harbour entrance.

At the fortress begins 'Gluttony Street'. The golden age of the famous restaurants of La Goulette is now past, but you still find here the colourful ambience of a harbour district, and can obtain fresh fish dishes and tasty Tunisian cuisine at reasonable prices. You can eat well in *Le Vert Galant* and in the *Brasserie l'An 2000*, both in the Avenue Franklin Roosevelt.

A free ferry for cars and people (bac) crosses the canal between 7 a.m. and 8.45 p.m., by which you can reach the eastern suburbs of Tunis.

Salammbô 16 km

This well kept health resort in fact forms part of Carthage, which is extensive enough to be served by five stops on the TGM suburban railway. Salammbô was once the headquarters of the Carthaginian admiralty. As a result of the silting up of the lagoon, little remains of the 600-m-long and 325-m-wide trading and naval port, with anchorage for 220 ships, which existed at that time. Today smart villas surround the two harbour basins, in the middle of which on the promontory stands the *Oceanographic Museum*. In addition to models of ships and seafaring equipment, it contains aquaria with all kinds of Mediterranean denizens, as well as displaying various methods of fishing.

Le Tophet, the place of worship of the goddess Tanit whose protection had to be bought by human sacrifice, lies near the Carthaginian harbour. Among flowers and bushes stand small gravestones sunk deep into the soft earth. They are in memory of the first-born of noble families who were sacrificed here to ensure victory in war or to abate natural catastrophes. More than 200 gravestones, often depicting the stylised sign of the goddess — the disc of Venus and the sickle of the moon — were found here in 1921, together with numerous urns of porous sandstone, frequently in the shape of little Egyptian or Greek

temples, containing the ashes of small children; some are to be found in the Bardo museum. The cult of the cruel goddess was taken very seriously; after a defeat at the hands of the Greeks, the people rebelled, maintaining that the rich had sacrificed the children of slaves instead of their own. Enraged by this deception, the goddess had arranged for the other side to be victorious. The sacrifice of the children is described most vividly by Gustave Flaubert in the novel *Salammbô,* which appeared in 1863 and is set in the period after the First Punic War.

Carthage 18 km

Once the centre of a world power, which even threatened the might of Rome (see page 14), Carthage today presents itself to the visitor as a bright and friendly place of white villas and splendid gardens. Up to the end of the last war little building was carried out by the locals at this scene of ancient drama. The Arabs seemed to avoid the blood-soaked ground; only Christians built houses and churches here. The new Tunisia has broken with the old taboo. Fear of the past has given way to a building boom. Even ex-President Bourguiba has his palace here.

The year 814 B.C. is taken as the date of the founding of Carthage by the Phoenicians on their wanderings from Tyre in the Lebanon (see page 14). From the name Kart Hadascht, meaning 'New Town', came the name Carthage, called *Punis* by the Romans. The centre of the rapidly growing town was formed by the 63-m-high *Byrsa Hill*, the peak of which was fortified and bore a temple to the god Esmun (who corresponded to the Roman Aesculapius).

Although Carthage lay in the centre of a well fortified peninsula, cut off from the mainland by three massive ramparts, it was conquered by the Romans in 146 B.C. and razed to the ground. The centre

Roman theatre and ruins, Carthage

of the Roman province of Africa in the first centuries A.D., and the second city of the Empire after Rome, Roman Carthage was again destroyed by the Mussulman-Arabic conquerors.

The stone of Carthage provided building material for the nascent city of Tunis and the Roman pillars found their way into the mosques.

After UNESCO had lodged an appeal to save ancient Carthage, research into the town gathered momentum.

📷 Compared with the actual city of Carthage, the ruins provide only a faint reminder and can convey but a vague impression of its historical importance.

We would strongly advise you to join a guided tour of Carthage. The knowledge of the taxi drivers is meagre and even the driver of one of the picturesque barouches cannot offer a historical tour of Carthage. He is more likely to tell you about Field Marshal Rommel and his Afrika Korps, and the bunkers they built on the Carthage coast!

However, if you merely wish to obtain a brief impression, then climb (or drive) to the top of Byrsa Hill, from which the *Cathédrale Saint Louis*, a decorative building from the turn of the century in the Byzantine-Moorish style, proudly looks down. From here you will have a view over remains from the Punic period towards the marshy former harbour of Carthage (see Salammbô).

Near the cathedral is the entrance to the *Musée National de Carthage*, the National Museum (opening times see page 92), which contains a collection of finds from Carthaginian, Roman, Christian and Islamic times.

If you have already seen one you can miss out the *Amphitheatre* — there are

Carthage

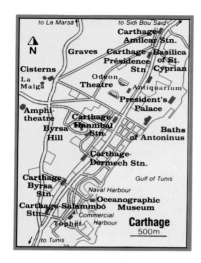

to La Marsa / to Sidi Bou Saïd
N
Carthage-Amilcar Stn.
Graves   Carthage-   Basilica
Présidence   of St.
Cisterns   Odéon   Stn   Cyprian
La Malga   Theatre
Antiquarium
President's Palace
Amphitheatre
Byrsa   Carthage-Hannibal   Baths of Antoninus
Hill   Stn.
Carthage-Dermech Stn.
Carthage-Byrsa Stn.   Gulf of Tunis
Naval Harbour
Oceanographic Museum
Carthage-Salammbô Stn.   Commercial Harbour
Tophet   **Carthage**
to Tunis   **500m**

better preserved ones to be seen.

On the other hand, the *Baths of Antoninus Pius* and the surrounding *Open-Air Museum* (opening times as the National Museum) are very impressive ancient sites. The Open-Air Museum can be reached through the imposing thermal baths, which occupy some 200 m of sea-shore. A 15-m-high column, with a Corinthian capital 1.8 m high and weighing 4 tonnes, testifies to the massive dimensions of these baths. Via some ruined steps the path leads through a gently climbing alleyway where ancient cisterns form small exhibition rooms for mosaics and fragments of statues.

200 m south of the Baths of Antoninus lies the *German Archaeological Park*. The showpiece is the Carthaginian sea-wall, covered in plaster. 100 m of the Roman sea fortifications have been exposed and restored.

On the other side of the Carthage — Sidi Bou Saïd road you can stroll through the ruins of a Roman village. The remains of a Roman *theatre*, which is still used from time to time, and of an *odeon*

(3rd c.) are to be seen. In the *Antiquarium*, a partially reconstructed Roman villa, are displayed finds from the surrounding area, and on the terrace 198 mosaics show scenes from Roman equestrian games (2nd and 3rd c.).

Further inland (some 500 m) you will come across the *Cisterns of La Malga*, a drinking-water depot consisting of immense pipes. This is where the Roman aqueduct from the Mountain of Zaghouan ends.

[R] In spite of the many visitors, Carthage is still a restful holiday resort. The streams of visitors have their fixed routes from one place of interest to the next.

[icon] The best beach is near the Hotel *Amilcar* on the hill of Sidi Bou Saïd (see entry).

     Boat hire.

[icon] In the direction of Sidi Bou Said.

[icon] In the ancient Carthage area you will be offered attractive imitations of oil lamps, masks and statuettes, all 'guaranteed genuine'. You can buy these imitations much more cheaply in the Bardo Museum in Tunis. Ninety-five per cent of the coins on offer are usually not genuine, just cleverly artificially aged — mostly in Italian and Lebanese workshops; or they are so badly preserved that they are not worth buying.

[icon] Pleasant places for meals, from the pizzeria to the exclusive *Neptune* on the coast, Rue Ibn Chabbat.

[icon] *Festival de Carthage* (see page 37). During the season performances by the Malouf groups (Tunisian folk music).

[icon] As soon as the sun has gone down you can go walking in the extensive parks of Carthage; as an alternative you can take short boat trips.

Sidi Bou Said 20 km

Bright, cube-shaped houses climb the 130-m-high hill. At the beginning of this century, Paul Klee and August Macke painted here. André Gide and Georges Bernanos found time to look, think and write. Today Sidi Bou Said is no longer a favourite haunt of artists and authors, even though on any evening you may still meet in the Moorish café some individualists engaged in writing, painting or film-making.

Sidi Bou Said was also founded by the Carthaginians. It is said that in the evenings a huge fire was lit on the top of the hill to 'light home' the Carthaginian ships. Centuries later a pious sage named Abou Said chose this hill as an ideal place for meditation. When he died in the year 1231 the place inherited his name. His grave in the shadow of the mosque is visited by many religious pilgrims.

In Sidi Bou Said you will still find the oriental charm of white domes, bright, walled steps and 'harem oriel windows' with wooden grilles on the houses. In the *Café des Nattes* (the 'straw matting' café) nothing has changed since Macke's visit. At one of the postcard stands look for a reproduction of the famous drawing of this café by Macke and you will see that everything looks just as it did in his time.

Most delightful of all, however, are the frequent glimpses of the blue sea below between the houses, walls, steps and trees.

Near the Café des Nattes a flight of steps leads through the park to the yacht station; you will have to face 265 steps. Coming back, it is better to use the gently climbing asphalt road along the coast past the Hotel Amilcar.

 The prettiest beach here — well kept and with every tourist comfort

Café des Nattes, Sidi Bou Said

Sidi Bou Said

— belongs to the *Amilcar* Hotel complex. However, in summer the beaches are overrun by people from the capital and are not exactly clean. You can walk down from the beautifully situated village on the hill to the beach below in half an hour.

     Through the Hotel *Amilcar* and at the yacht station.

 On the steep slope of Sidi Bou Said.

  Hotel *Amilcar*.

 Fish and seafood: *Dar Zarrouk* on the hill; *Le Pirate* Garden Restaurant by the yacht station; *Floating Restaurant* in a converted ship.

 Hotel *Amilcar*.

 La Barraka.

At the end of August the religious festival of *El Kharja* is celebrated.

La Marsa 22 km
The TGM suburban railway ends here. The Arabs called the place *Marsa Roum*, the 'Christian Marsa', because Coptic Christians from Egypt had settled here. In the 19th c. the little town became the favourite summer residence of the rich families of Tunis. The Beys also spent the summer here; their bathing pavilion, standing on stilts in the sea, is not used today. The palaces and villas stretch as far as the elegant seaside resort of Gammarth, some 2 km away.

At the entrance to the town, in well guarded parkland, stands the government guest house, the *Palais Es-Saada*. Inland, behind the subway, we find Saf-Saf Square with its *Hafsid Mosque* and the well known Moorish *Café Saf-Saf*, in the friendly, shaded courtyard of which a patient dromedary drives the wheel of a well, said to date from the time of the Hafsids.

 The free bathing beach immediately near the town is neglected, but leads to the fashionable suburb of Gammarth (2 km).

Au Bon Vieux Temps, Rue Abou El Kacem Chebbi.

Gammarth 24 km
The wide bay of Gammarth is slowly being built up with hotels of the luxury class. With the help of Arab oil dollars, buildings are being erected, enlarged and modernised. Anyone who settles here is dependent on his own transport. There are no longer any shops in between the luxury villas and sprawling hotel complexes. If you want to buy anything you have to drive to neighbouring La Marsa. On the other hand the beach part of Gammarth is known for its large number of excellent restaurants.

In a wonderful setting on the hill which towers over the Gammarth beaches, a giant and extremely luxurious hotel complex is being built which is aimed mainly at holidaymakers from the Arab countries.

Through a eucalyptus forest, past the Bay of Apes (although there are no longer any apes), a 4-km-long main road leads to Raouad.

The beaches are the most beautiful in the Gulf, a broad landscape of dunes of fine sand. In summer it gets very busy here, especially at the weekend. However, as the stretches of sand are very long and quite broad, it is usually possible to get sufficient air on the hotel beaches not accessible to the general public — even though the atmosphere is lively and noisy!

 Autumn is quiet and particularly beautiful in Gammarth. The weather remains quite warm right into October.

 In the north, near the cape.

 Arranged through the *Abou Nawas* hotel.

 At the hotels' own courts.

 In some hotels.

 The *Hammam de la République*, near the three filling stations on the road into Tunis, is the nicest sauna in the Tunis region.

♫ *Galaxy* in the hotel *La Tour Blanche*, jazz in the *Yacht Club* of the *Abou Nawas* hotel.

⊗ *Le Selmia* in the *Abou Nawas* hotel.

✗ By the sea in the Raouad direction: *Le Pêcheur, Les Coquillages, Les Dunes*. Evening meal with folk music entertainment in the *Select Club* by the sea.

🚶 By the beach and on the hills. Worth visiting is the French military cemetery (*Cimetière militaire français*), on the high ground between Gammarth and La Marsa. The depressing nature of the memorials is more than compensated for by the singular beauty of the surroundings; from here, especially at sunset, you have an enchanting view over the sea. On a clear day you can pick out not only Cap Bon, but also Cap Farina to the north-west and the island of Zimbra in the north-east. Near the cemetery are Jewish graves estimated to be 2000 years old, the hollows of which

gave the mountain its name *Djebel Khaoui* (the 'hollowed-out mountain').

Raouad 28 km
Raouad means endless beaches and dunes. The area, which is some 4 km long, has been opened up by means of a motor road which runs parallel to the beach. As a day visitor you can also avail yourself of the wide range of sporting activities offered by the Cap Carthage and Dar Naouar hotels.

Near the small town of Raouad the road swings off again towards Tunis. You have been almost all the way round the salt-lake of *Sebkhet El Ariana* and have reached the main Tunis — Biserta road.

In the hotels *Cap Carthage* and *Dar Naouar*.

Suburbs east of Tunis
Ez Zahra and Hammam-Lif 6 km
At one time Ez Zahra, south-east of Tunis, was a purely French suburb. The picture has changed, and the Tunisian middle classes have bought property here.

Ez Zahra joins Hammam-Lif, which grew up thanks mainly to Djebel Bou Kornine (the 'two-horned mountain') and the hot, therapeutic waters found inside it. The Romans long ago realised the value of the streams flowing out of the mountain, but it was the Turkish Beys who first constructed swimming baths here and built themselves palaces on the mountain slopes. The suburbs of Tunis end at Hammam-Lif. You then see the first vegetable plantations; vineyards and olive groves appear, and then a few more factories.

🚶 2½ hours on the Bou Kornine (15 minutes by car).

Borj Cedria 28 km
In the extreme corner of the bay in the Gulf of Tunis can be found some upper

middle class hotels; a riding club has its home here too.

🚌 Excursions from Tunis

Some of the many things worth seeing in the country can be reached most easily from the capital itself; the simplest way is to join a group. Coach excursions, including some lasting several days, are offered by the larger hotels. Multilingual guides accompany the groups.

Hire cars are as expensive as in Europe and public transport — trains, cross-country buses or group taxis — mostly serves the modern places, not historical sites.

Tunis — Utica — Ghar El Melh — Raf Raf — Metline — El Alia — Biserta — Tunis (190 km)

Utica. The harbour of Utica has been silted up for a long time and the open sea cannot be seen. In Utica, once an important Carthaginian port, the Romans landed in the Third Punic War, but Utica escaped destruction, for the town decided just in time to co-operate with Rome. Worth seeing from the Punic period are the *Necropolis*, with graves up to 3 m in length, some of them covered with monoliths, and remains of Punic pillars and Roman mosaics. The harbour wall has also survived the centuries, while the sea has receded several kilometres during that period.

Ghar El Melh (the salt hole). The best potatoes in Tunisia grow in this area. The small, fortified harbour of Ghar El Melh was formerly notorious for its three fortress-like prisons. The massive bulwarks indeed withstood Admiral Blake, when in 1655 he and the British fleet tried to free some Englishmen held prisoner here. One of these buildings served as a prison right up to the

seventies; today some poor families live in the windowless cells.

Passing the old fishing harbour you reach the beach. The only domed building on Cap Farina is the grave of the saint Ali El Mekki, to whom this romantic section of the coast is dedicated. Within the next few years a gigantic holiday town with 16,000 hotel beds and an Arab Disneyland are expected to be built here.

Raf Raf is as famous for its picturesque streets and old women in traditional costume as it is for its superior wine grapes. The rich of Tunis have built holiday villas here. On pleasant summer days the beach is overcrowded and the approach roads jammed with traffic.

Metline, the pretty little town built in terraces on the hillside, is worth a visit.

El Alia is an Andalusian village on a mountain massif. The Moriscos, Arab migrants returning from Andalusia, settled here in the 17th c.

20 km further on you reach Biserta (see page 49). It is 66 km back to Tunis on the fast road.

Tunis — Testour — Teboursouk — Dougga — Tunis (230 km)

You cross the Medjerda River, the largest river in Tunisia, at Medjez El Bab.

Testour is the centre of the Andalusian returning emigrants. The mosque, built in the first half of the 17th c. in the Spanish Renaissance style, is worth seeing, as the minaret is fitted with a sundial — a rarity in the Islamic world. In Testour, too, is the grave of the Rabbi Fradj Chaoua. According to the votive tablets a walk along the wall can keep the pious Tunisian Jew free from sickness.

Right: Dougga

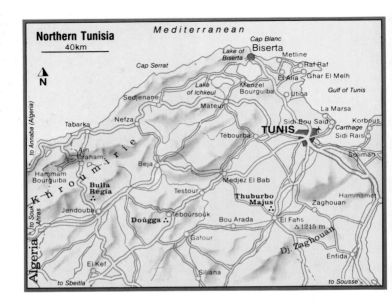

Teboursouk (pop. 11,000) lies 500 m high on a slope. You can visit the remains of a Byzantine castle, a Roman gateway and a Roman cemetery.

Dougga is one of the most important excavation sites in the Roman province of Africa. Here you can get a good idea of what an ancient town may have looked like. Way back in Punic times mention was made of Dougga, of its healthy situation (alt. 500 m) and of its size. Its most prosperous period was under Roman administration. Unlike most other ancient towns in North Africa, however, neither the collapse of the Roman Empire nor the Arab conquest meant the complete end for Dougga. It remained inhabited.

Purely Punic relics are rare, even in Dougga! You will not fail to see a 21-m-high restored Libyan-Punic Mausoleum to the south, which is the tomb of a Numidian prince from the 2nd c. B.C. The inscription on the mausoleum was taken to the British Museum in the middle of the last century to have the ancient Libyan alphabet deciphered. Also from Punic times is the defensive wall flanked by two towers. Everything else was left by the Romans.

Coming from the Teboursouk direction, on the right (north of the entrance to the site of the ruins) lies the *Temple of Saturn*, erected in A.D. 195 for the Emperor Septimus Severus. The *Theatre* at the entrance was endowed by a patrician in A.D. 166, and today in summer is still the scene of classical drama during the Festival of Carthage. Along a cobbled street past the *Pietas Augusta Temple* you will come to a square with a 9-m-wide representation of a compass, which was chiselled into the paving in A.D. 192, and to the *Capitol* with its *Temple* dedicated to the gods Jupiter, Juno and Minerva. This temple, with its well preserved gable relief, is considered one of the most beautiful buildings of its kind in North Africa. To the west are the *Triumphal Arch of Severus Alexander* (3rd c.) and the contemporary *Temple of Juno Caelestis*. In the southern part of the site, near the Libyan-Punic Mausoleum, was once the aristocratic villa area.

A bit of everyday life in the old town is to be seen in the latrines of the public conveniences with running water, or in the remains of the bath houses.

For the return journey to Tunis we recommend taking the same road that you came on. If you take two days, you can include a visit to *Bulla Regia* (see below) in your plans. In that case the beautifully situated Ain Draham (Hotel *Les Chênes*) is recommended.

Tunis — Bulla Regia — Tunis (330 km)

Going via Medjez El Bab and Beja (pop. 35,000), which is in a fertile area and where remains of a Byzantine town wall can be seen, drive to Jendouba and then turn off in the direction of Ain Draham.

The green landscape at Dougga

Bulla Regia. The ruins which still exist cannot be compared with the magnificence of Dougga or Sbeitla; a serious earthquake laid waste the historical monuments. The interest of this ancient town lies in the fact that it was laid out underground. The winters here are cold, with a lot of snow (Ain Draham, about 30 km away, is a winter sports area), and the summers hot. Living underground guaranteed pleasantly even temperatures.

Behind the entrance gate to the ruined town a *cistern,* remains of a *Byzantine castle, baths* and the remains of two early Christian *basilicas* can still be seen.

You then come first of all to the district of villas and palaces which date from the 3rd c. and which bear witness to the wealth of the inhabitants of the time; there are the *Palace of the Peacock,* the *Palace of the Hunt* and the *Palace of Fishing,* etc., each named after the superb mosaics which have been found in these palaces. The most impressive mosaic is in the *Palace of Amphitrite*. The head of Amphitrite is formed from particularly fine small mosaics. The eyes made of precious stones have been stolen.

Tunis — Zaghouan (Djebel Zaghouan) — Thuburbo Majus — Tunis (150 km).

On the motorway to Hammamet you turn off (after 5 km) in the direction of

Dougga   100 m

1 Libyan-Punic Mausoleum
2 Temple of Saturn
3 Theatre
4 Pieta Augusta Temple
5 Square of the Compass
6 Capitol
7 Triumphal Arch of Severus Alexander
8 Temple of Juno Caelestis

Thuburbo Majus

Kairouan. After about 30 km a road goes off to the left. Passing the modern thermal bath of *Djebel Oust* (with hotel) you come to Zaghouan, lying at the foot of the 1295-m-high *Djebel Zaghouan*.

Zaghouan (pop. 10,000) is a pretty little town. From here a minor road (signposted 'Temple des Eaux') snakes its way up the hill (2 km). You come to a café-restaurant with a small car park; by the side of the rocks is the *Nymphaeum*, a giant water basin near the spring from which the Romans in Carthage conveyed their drinking water across the mighty aqueduct. The Water Temple was built by the Emperor Hadrian. Giant statues once stood in the twelve niches. A pleasant walk can be enjoyed in the adjoining wood.

 Hotel *Les Nymphes*, prettily situated near the Nymphaeum.

Returning via Zaghouan follow the signs to *El Fahs* and after 25 km you reach Thuburbo Majus on a hill.

Thuburbo Majus. There was a Punic settlement here in the 5th c. B.C., and at the time of Christ the Romans arrived. The town prospered as a result of grain growing and reached its peak in the 2nd c. Its decline began with the invasion of the Vandals. Then came the Byzantines who attributed little importance to the town in spite of its favourable situation. The Arabs in the 7th c. probably found only a largish village which was soon abandoned, became forgotten and was not rediscovered until 1875. Only a fifth of the extensive town has been uncovered.

When visiting the ruins you will see in the northern part (near the entrance) the square Forum with the *Capitol Temple*, standing on massive foundations.

On the north-east side of the 2400-sq.-m Forum remains of the *Curia*, the town hall, can be recognised; on the opposite side it joins the *Temple of Mercury* and at the southern point of the Forum lies the *Market*, probably not sited here till the 2nd c. 50 m south-east from there we come to the scarcely discernible remains of the *Winter Baths*. More worth seeing are the cold, warm and hot rooms of the *Summer Baths*, once luxuriously furnished with marble and mosaic floors, and found behind the *Palaestra*, the sports hall. Of the porticos which once lined the Palaestra, the *Colonnade of the Petronii* has survived, named after the family of the merchant Petronius Felix who endowed the site in 225. On the south-eastern side of the Palaestra can be seen the marble floor of the *Temple of Aesculapius* and the remains of a *Byzantine church*. Through the adjoining area of ruins you come to the *Baal-Tanit Temple*.

In *Thuburbo Majus*, also, uniquely beautiful sunsets are to be enjoyed.

Biserta (French Bizerte)
Pop. 95,000

From Tunis a well constructed road (60 km) leads through hilly, fairly green countryside, planted with cereals, fruit and olive trees. With a shared taxi (*louage*) you can cover the distance in an hour.

Its dominant position at the narrowest part of the Mediterranean once made Biserta a naval base comparable with Gibraltar. The French finally relinquished it in 1963, since when the old garrison town has been slowly converted into an industrial centre. Tunisia's only oil refinery to date is to be found here and a few kilometres inland is the country's biggest blast-furnace, El Fouladh.

A Phoenician colony as long ago as 1000 B.C. and called in antiquity Diarrythus, Biserta was conquered in the 4th c. by Agathocles, the tyrant of Syracuse, and later became a colony of the Roman Empire. In 661 the Arabs arrived, named the place *Benzerte* and,

Biserta, the Old Port

making it their temporary royal seat, embellished it with palaces and gardens. In the 16th c. the Turks used the well protected bay as a hide-out for their much feared Corsair ships.

Sightseeing

Biserta, the fourth largest town in Tunisia, lies — as you come from the direction of Tunis — beyond a wide canal built in olden times. It connects the Biserta inland lake with the open sea. The canal, which is spanned by a bascule bridge, serves as an international port. Traversing the New Town, which was built during the period of the French protectorate, you continue from the bridge to the *Old Harbour* (Vieux Port), the *Market* and the covered *Fish Market*. Here life proceeds in the traditional way, with no signs of the industrialisation of Biserta. Long-serving fishing smacks with painted sails and lanterns rock gently near the boats of the coral divers and lobster catchers. Near the harbour entrance rises the imposing silhouette of the *Kasbah* (13th — 14th c.); to the north of it the *Andalusian Quarter* reminds us of the re-migration of the Moors from Spain at the end of the 16th c. Many of the inhabitants of the latticed houses are said still to possess the keys of the palaces which their forefathers had to leave behind in Andalusia 400 years ago. Thus in Tunisia people do not speak of 'castles in the air' but dream of 'castles in Spain'.

Some 3 km from the town centre the coastal road known as the *Corniche* runs through what is in part a most elegant and quiet beach area with some modern hotels.

 In the north-east at rocky *Cap Blanc*.

 S At the *Club Nautique* at the corner of the canal entrance and Boul. Habib Bou Guetfa. Cap Blanc offers good sport for sub-aqua fishermen. There are particularly fine

Tabarka, coral jewellery

crayfish to be found off the island of *Galite*, where Habib Bourguiba was interned by the French. A steamer sails to the island once a week; the Club Nautique organises further trips. There is sailing on the sea and on the Biserta lake.

    Facilities at the hotels

U Horse-riding can be arranged through hotel reception.

Arts and Craft Centre (ONAT) at the Old Harbour; wrought-iron work, embroidery, ceramics.

i *Office de Tourisme:* 1 Rue de Constantinople.

To the animal sanctuary on the *Lake of Ichkeul* (25 km). Many species of birds spend the winter here; water-buffalo, porcupines and jackals live on the marshes.

It is about 30 km to Utica (see page 44).

Tabarka Pop. 10,000.

At the north-western corner of Tunisia — some 170 km from Biserta and about the same distance from Tunis — can be found the picturesque and tranquil little port of Tabarka at the mouth of the Kebir and only 15 km from the Algerian border. For centuries Tabarka has been the chief harbour for coral divers, but today it is also a port for the export of cork.

The mountainous hinterland, the *Khroumirie*, is rich in forest and wildlife. Here grows the mighty cork-oak, and in its shade the bruyère bush from the root nodules of which are shaped the bowls of smokers' pipes.

On the island, which is connected to the mainland by a causeway, stands an old Genoese castle. The Italian royal families of Lomellini and Grimaldi, a branch of the house of Monaco, were attracted to Tabarka by the lovely red coral, and it is said that in 1542 they exchanged their prisoner, the pirate chieftain Dragut, for the island. The island became a Genoese Christian outpost and in 1741 it had some 1200 inhabitants. The Genoese were a thorn in the flesh of the then ruler of Tunis, Ali Pascha Bey. He occupied the island and sold the inhabitants as slaves.

Tabarka and its hinterland are increasingly favoured by those who like an active holiday.

 Sandy beach broken by curious needle-cliffs.

Hotel *Club El Moriane*.

  In the Khroumirie Mountains.

 Quail (end of September) and wild boar (October to December). Organised hunting expeditions.

 Local restaurants. Specialities: crayfish, bouillabaisse (a rich fish stew) and roast wild boar, etc., in the hunting season.

Tabarka

 The *Coral Festival*, at the end of May, offers the best opportunities of going out to sea with the coral divers; exhibitions and sale of coral jewellery. July/August *International Festival* with Tunisian folk singers and young artists from all over the world.

 Coral jewellery, Bruyère pipes, wood-carvings, Khroumirie carpets (black-white-beige).

Ain Draham (20 km). This mountain village, at an altitude of 800 m and set in the midst of woodland, looks quite European with its red tiled roofs. Ain Draham, in English the 'silver spring', is renowned as a hot spa for treating illnesses of the nose, larynx and ears. Snow falls here in winter.

Wild boar hunting. Organised hunting safaris.

Les Chênes, prettily situated in the forest.

Office de Tourisme in the town centre.

After driving 12 km in the direction of the Algerian border, you come to the *Hammam Bourguiba Thermal Baths*, where ex-President Bourguiba frequently took the cure. From Ain Draham it is 35 km to Bulla Regia (see page 47).

Hammamet

Cap Bon

Hilly Cap Bon is the fruit and vegetable garden of Tunisia. Ancient Rome obtained its food supplies here and today it provides central Europeans with some of their early vegetables. The lovely garden landscape, with its huge orange-plantations and vineyards — sweet lemons grow here too — stretches as far as the apparently endless sandy beaches which line the cape. No wonder that a third of all Tunisia's hotel beds are to be found here in the Hammamet/Nabeul region. Yet nowhere do the wide beaches and extensive parks attached to the hotels give one that depressingly cramped feeling that is experienced in many Mediterranean holiday centres.

Hammamet Pop. 30,000

The old town lies only 60 km south-east of Tunis. For a day's excursion from or to Tunis the frequent buses (in Tunis from the *Gare Routière* Southern Coach Station, on the edge of the city) or a shared taxi are best. Hammamet was probably built 500 years ago close to, and partly with stone from, old Roman ruins. The town possesses no special ancient monuments, nor any great historical highlights. Perhaps that is in its favour, for it still retains the quiet charm of simple life.

The oriental colourfulness of the *Medina*, which today is still completely surrounded by a wall, attracted French artists to Hammamet at the turn of the century. The *Main Gate of the Town Wall* dates from its original foundation. The *Great Mosque* has a simple but over 500-year-old minaret.

The *Kasbah*, which developed from the 12th—15th c., stands in solitary splendour on a giant rock on the beach. In the Kasbah can be found a café, with a magnificent view, a saint's grave, and the only *Ram-fighting Museum* in the world. The 'Beliomarchie', the horn-fight between two rams, is a bloodless pleasure enjoyed by the Tunisians, who breed fighting rams as the Spaniards breed bulls.

Near the Kasbah the fishermen pull their boats up on to the beach. Fish are still caught by means of the 'Lampara' method introduced by the Romans — the fisherman goes out in the dark and entices them with large carbide lamps or headlights.

The *holiday town* begins near the old town, where lie the gardens and villas of the wealthy, and stretches for a long way. In practice various hotels have combined to form their own small holiday towns. Boutiques, restaurants and cafés have been set up and you have to force yourself to leave these enclaves, which offer everything. In the hotel gardens, most of which have elegantly equipped swimming pools, flourish greenery and a profusion of flowers, producing the mixed scents and colours of oleander and jasmine, geranium and hibiscus, orange and cactus blooms, growing beneath the shadow of cypress, palm, pine and eucalyptus trees.

The hotels also look after your entertainment. There are discothèques, nightclubs and folk evenings; party games are arranged and excursions on dromedaries or by boat are organised. For young people the evening meeting place is the modern entertainment

Decorative door, Hammamet

quarter opposite the Kasbah. Hammamet is ideal for those who like to join in and have fun.

At the beginning of the hotel complexes there is a small rocky area; then follow flat beaches of fine sand, which stretch over several kilometres to the south and in the north merge with the beaches of Nabeul.

     Facilities for watersports are abundant in all hotels. Do not hesitate to go to a neighbouring hotel for something which your own hotel cannot offer.

Each hotel can arrange for the hire of horses, dromedaries and donkeys.

Some hotels have their own facilities, and also have arrangements with neighbouring hotels.

Cap Bon Peninsula

Zembra Island

Ghar El Kebir

El Haouaria

Sidi Daoud

Gulf of Tunis

Kerkouane

Kelibia

Korbous

Menzel Temime

Sidi Rais

Soliman Menzel Bou Zelfa

Korba

Grombalia

Maamourca

Nabeul

Hammamet

to Tunis

to Sousse

20 km

N

🏊 Most of the hotel swimming pools are heated.

🛵 At the southern exit from Hammamet on the arterial road going in the direction of Sousse.

🛝 There are children's playgrounds in various hotels.

🎵 🍷 In the hotels and in the entertainment centre opposite the Kasbah.

🍴 There are restaurants here for every taste and purse. For traditional food with oriental music and dancing you should eat in *Chez Achour*.

Nabeul Pop. 40,000

The small capital of Cap Bon, 12 km north of Hammamet, is a centre of Tunisian arts and crafts. Not only in the *Centre d'Artisanat* in the main street is the work of potters, embroiderers and basket-makers displayed, but ceramic tiles, statuettes and pots in all colours and shapes can be seen everywhere in the souks and in colourful little courtyards. Pottery was made here in Roman times and antique patterns still survive in the shapes and decorations of many jugs, vases and dishes. Side by side with them are also to be found the traditional Arab patterns based on geometric shapes and letters.

You can have a tile or vase made with your name — or any other word! — inscribed on it in Arabic script which is very decorative. They take about a week to produce. If you say your name slowly and precisely any Tunisian can write it down for you. As a check get another Tunisian to read it back to you. With this slip of paper in your hand you can go into any pottery shop, but haggle over the price in advance.

As well as for ceramics Nabeul is well known for its perfumes. Here the ethereal oil of the wild orange, called *Neroli*, is extracted; this is always found in Eau de Cologne.

The Roman *Neapolis* used to lie right by the sea. In the meantime the sand has moved the place 1–2 km inland and created new land for the hotels which extend all along the beach. It is quieter here than in Hammamet.

The largest hotel complex is the holiday-village of *Lido-Nabeul*, which, with its hotel, bungalows, solarium, own electrical generator, purifying plant for germ-free water and its own large butcher's shop, is aimed mainly at families with children; the guests can do their own cooking, the beach is flat and there is also a nursery for the children.

🏖 The beaches are well maintained and equipped with all necessities.

Vary from hotel to hotel.

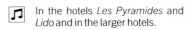
In the hotels *Les Pyramides* and *Lido* and in the larger hotels.

Offered by each hotel. Worth seeing is the camel and animal market which is combined with the weekly market on Fridays.

 *Office de Tourisme*, Avenue Taieb Mahiri.

North of Nabeul, on the stretch of road to Korba 18 km distant, stands the village of *Maamourca*, which has a charming bungalow complex by the sea with swimming pool, restaurant, discothèque and nightclub.

Korba Pop. 22,000
The town gets its charm from its terraced layout on the bank of the Ouëd Bou Eddine, and from the original shape of its houses. Only the ruined cisterns of an aqueduct remain to remind us of the Roman *Curubis*. On the splendid beach is a village of the Club Méditerranée, which meets every need of the (younger) sports fan.

Pottery, Nabeul

All the way round Cap Bon
Coach excursions to Cap Bon are offered by all the tourist hotels on the Gulf of Hammamet. Going via Nabeul, Korba and Menzel Temime you arrive at:

Kelibia (Pop. 25,000; 58 km from Hammamet). A massive fortress crowns an 82-m-high hill. Punic, Roman and Byzantine remains have been found near the fortress. The town, lying at the foot of the hill, was founded in 309 B.C. by Sicilian Greeks. Scipio destroyed it at the same time as Carthage. Kelibia is renowned for its excellent dry wine *Muscat sec de Kelibia* and its outstanding fish restaurants at the harbour.

    Hotel *Mansoura*.

Kerkouane lies 9 km further north. Here in the coastal area you will find the best-preserved *Punic town* in Africa (6th—5th c. B.C.). The ruins were first discovered in 1952 and the excavations are far from complete. Kerkouane must have been a prosperous town for nowhere else have so many private baths been found.

El Haouaria, 25 km from Kerkouane, lies at the northern point of the cape. From the lighthouse hill on a clear night you can see the lights winking from Sicily, 140 km away. In El Haouaria, late May/early June, the *Festival of the Falconers* takes place. It is true that there are seldom falcons to admire, only sparrowhawks, but this small difference takes nothing away from the excitement of this show, which admittedly ends rather cruelly: to judge the best bird of prey, sparrows are released, and the sparrowhawks seldom fail to catch their living target.

Ghar El Kebir is 2 km away. The giant Roman stone quarries, which provided building material for the construction of Roman Carthage, appear like large

Sousse market

caves. Soldiers of the German Afrika Korps retreated here before being taken prisoner. In some caves live rare species of bats. You cannot visit these caves.

Sidi Daoud is a further 12 km on the northern side of the cape. It is actually a ghost town which only comes to life in May and June, when the tuna fish come near the coast to spawn. Wide nets, consisting of chambers which get smaller and smaller, are hung from the boats; they end in a funnel-shaped 'chamber of death' (Chambre de Mort). When the fish reach the last net-chamber there begins, to the accompaniment of melancholy singing, the *Mantanza* — the killing of the tuna. If you have strong nerves and wish to go on one of the boats, you will need a pass from the *Office de Pêche* in Tunis (opposite the TGM Railway Station at the end of Avenue Habib Bourguiba; open only in the morning).

Korbous, a small colourful spa in a rocky bay, is 50 km further on. Up to the beginning of the eighties it was still little known. It is now said that Korbous is to become an international seaside resort. The Romans long ago took their steam baths here and you should do the same, either in the *Spa Rooms* or in the popular Hammam. Ask for the spring *Ain Atrous* (1.5 km outside), which shoots its water, heated to some 50°C, into the Gulf of Tunis, thus making a warm bathe in the sea possible even at the cold times of the year.

     The hotels *Ain Oktor* and *Les Sources* offer thermal cures.

Via the small fishing town of *Sidi Rais*, famous for its wine, we return to Hammamet and Nabeul.

The Sahel

Between the Djebel Zaghouan in the north, the Tell Atlas mountain range in the west, the coastal land in the east and the fringe of the Sahara with the great salt lake in the south, lie the high plateaux and lowland plains of central Tunisia. The Tunisians call this region Sahel, which is 'shoreland' in English, and thus means that eastern coastal area where the undulating hills sweep down to the seashore.

First of all a broad belt of olive trees extends over many kilometres — millions of trees, producing one of Tunisia's chief exports, olive oil. Further south the only thing that still grows in the semi-Saharan climate is the hard alfa grass, rich in cellulose; it is an important raw material in the paper industry, as well as being used in numerous trades for making rope, bags, baskets, hats and prayer-mats. Vegetables are cultivated along the coast and harvested several times in the year.

A quarter of the Tunisian population lives in the Sahel, which contains the two largest towns after Tunis, the important industrial town of Sfax and the capital of the Sahel, Sousse. The harbours of these two towns helped to boost the area economically and culturally in olden times and made fishing the second branch of the economy after olive oil. However, it is not only Sousse and Sfax which have something to offer to the visitor in this region; in the Sahel and on its western fringe you will find such famous and historically significant places as El Djem, Sbeitla, Maktar and Kairouan.

Sousse Pop. 85,000

This popular holiday resort lies 140 km from Tunis, at the most southerly end of the Gulf of Hammamet. The charm of this town lies in the combination of the still traditionally Arab life in the Medina with the flair of a growing resort. Easy to reach by road, many excursions can be made from Sousse.

The Phoenicians built a harbour in Sousse (11th c. B.C.), which they called Hadrametum, many years before the founding of Carthage. It escaped destruction by the victorious Romans in the 3rd Punic War because, like Utica, it had renounced Carthage in time. The Roman Emperor Trajan later renamed the place *Ulpia Trajana Augusta Frugifera Hadrumetina*, the Vandals called it *Hunericopolis* and the Byzantines *Justinianopolis*. The Arabs gave the port the name of *Susa*, which became the Sousse of today. An extensive European new town grew up during the time of the French Protectorate. Much was destroyed during the Second World War; reconstruction took the form of modernisation and was not to the town's disadvantage.

Sightseeing

A central point from which you can easily find your way is the *Farhat-Hached Square* with the statue of Habib Bourguiba on horseback. This is where the *louages* (shared taxis) from the north arrive; this is also where you can hire a horse-drawn carriage for an evening trip in the cool sea breeze, and where the old and new towns meet. On the main street — Avenue Habib Bourguiba — which leads from Farhat-Hached Square to the beach promenade, Boulevard Hedi Chaker, you will find the best shops: modern craft boutiques, pretty cafés and good restaurants. The hotel zone begins at Boulevard Hedi Chaker and continues as far as Port El Kantaoui, 10 km away.

The Medina. Leaving Farhat-Hached Square in the opposite direction, you pass through a wide gap in the town wall, built in 859, and enter the skilfully restored Medina with a row of buildings dating back to the 11th and even 10th centuries. Of the original six gates in the town wall only three remain.

Directly behind the wall stands the *Great Mosque* (9th c.) with its low

Wall of the Medina, Sousse

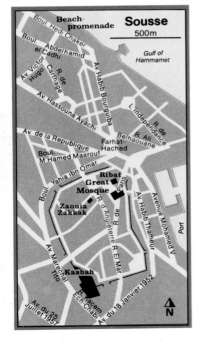

minaret. The inner courtyard, lined with arcaded walkways, can be visited (8 a.m.–2 p.m. daily except Friday). The mosque, which originally served to defend the harbour, has been rebuilt several times. In 1675 it was given a prayer-hall with thirteen aisles.

At the time they were built the mosque and the *Ribat* (fortified monastery), a little to the north-west, stood right by the harbour. The present-day harbour was not constructed until the 19th and 20th centuries.

The Ribat of Sousse, dating from the 8th c., ranks as the most important secular building in North Africa of this early Arab period. In simple cloistered cells in this fortress lived the soldiers of Allah, and they had to defend the port as well as their religion. They had to be prepared at any time to suffer a martyr's death in the struggle against the Infidels.

The *Zaouia Zakkak*, situated south-west of the Ribat, with its Medrese (an Islamic high school), dates from the Turkish period (18th c.) as is indicated by its richly decorated octagonal minaret.

The Medina, measuring 500 × 700 m, is dominated by the *Kasbah*, built in the 8th c.; its fortress has been strengthened many times over the centuries. The castle tower is 30 m high but if you climb it you will be 77 m above sea-level and will have a splendid all-round view.

The *Museum* in the Kasbah, with its rich collection of Punic, Roman and early Christian finds, ranks as the most important after the Bardo Museum. By the skilful way in which it is arranged the large Roman mosaic collection documents the different styles, from the earlier geometric compositions to the large narrative mosaic pictures of the 2nd and 3rd centuries. The museum is open 9 a.m.–noon and 3–6.30 p.m., except Mondays and public holidays; in winter it closes at 5.30 p.m.

2 km to the west outside the town we come to the *Catacombs*. The Christians

Above: The Great Mosque, Sousse
Right: Sousse Medina

of Sousse interred their dead here from the 2nd to the 4th centuries. The 15,000 graves in 240 rows were not discovered until 1888. The only ones you can visit are the *Catacombs of the Good Shepherd*, named after a mosaic found there, with 6000 graves in rows of caves 1½ km long. It is wise to take a powerful torch with you. The art objects found in the graves are on display in the Kasbah Museum (opening times above).

From the north the kilometre-long beach extends as far as the Sousse harbour basin. From the hotels on

Avenue Habib Bourguiba it is only a stone's throw to the beach.

 On hire at the yacht club.

 Can be hired through the hotels.

   At the hotels.

 Lido at the harbour; fish specialities.

 In the large hotels.

 Office de Tourisme, 1 Av. Habib Bourguiba.

The train called 'La Tortue Blanche' runs between Sousse (Boujaâfar beach-promenade) and Port El Kantaoui. During the journey the customs and traditions of the region are explained in English and other languages.

Monastir beach

Port El Kantaoui

The 'first garden-port of the Mediterranean', as Port El Kantaoui (10 km north of Sousse) is called, is a holiday town in itself. Hotels of various price levels are grouped around an Andalusian-style village in which apartments can be rented. In the harbour lie boats from many countries. The holidaymaker can find everything he needs here — post office, bank, supermarket, bars, discos, restaurants, cafés, travel agents, car-hire, excursions in sailing or motor boats — even a cinema in an old caravel.

    Pedal boats.

 Diving school.

    18-hole course.

Monastir Pop. 36,000

South of Sousse lies the little town of Monastir, which today, with its golden beach of *Skanès* and its international airport situated inland, has grown into a tourist centre. A yachting harbour, a new golf course and some very luxurious hotels entice the discriminating holidaymaker.

 Monastir, called *Rus Penna* in Punic times, gets its name from an early Christian 'monasterium' (monastery) which was located here and which was later named El Monastir by the Arabs. Caesar assembled his troops here before leaving to conquer Egypt and the beautiful Cleopatra. In 796 an Abbasid owner of the town had a massive Ribat built, in order to be able to defend the land of Ifriquia against the Infidels.

📷 Sightseeing

In spite of many additions and alterations

Port El Kantaoui

The Ribat in Monastir

to the building, the fortified monastery on the coast road, now serving as a film and theatre backdrop and housing a museum of Islamic art, is still one of the most magnificent fortified structures of the Islamic world. A tall circular tower rises above the ramparts, which are not, as is more usual, in the centre of the town. The *Great Mosque*, dating from the 9th to the 11th century, stands modestly nearby.

In the Medina much has been restored and new buildings in the Moorish style have been added, so that it appears well maintained. In the side streets, however, the old Medina way of life still goes on. Some mosques have minarets worthy of note; the *Bourguiba Mosque* in the Rue de l'Indépendance, with its 41-m-high octagonal minaret, was built as recently as 1963. Also in the Medina is a *Museum of Traditional Costume* which is worth seeing.

Monastir was the birthplace of ex-President Habib Bourguiba. You can admire the house in which he was born in *Rue Trabelsia*, as well as the mausoleum with a golden dome which he had built in the cemetery between the Medina and the harbour, and his magnificent marble residence in Skanès.

 Together with the very elegant neighbouring town of Skanès, some 6–7 km to the north, which possesses a number of really stylish hotels, Monastir has some of the most varied beaches in Tunisia and these have been imaginatively developed. Below the coast road are rows of bathing huts, with the massive Ribat towering above them.

 Pedal, rowing and motor boats can be hired during the season; also trips in fishing boats.

  Off the Monastir cliffs; diving school on the island (L'Ile).

 In Skanès and Monastir.

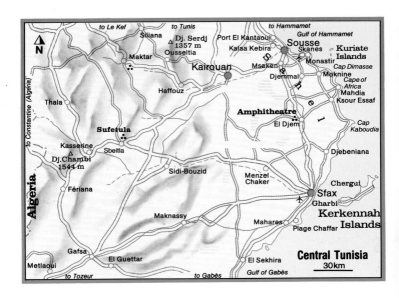

Mosque of Bourguiba, Monastir

On courses at the *Skanès Palace* hotel; also on the beaches.

Facilities only at certain hotels.

Le Flamand Rose, Route Touristique, and at the yacht harbour.

Les Grottes on the Monastir promenade.

At the hotels.

In the summer, folk concerts are held in the Ribat.

Office de Tourisme, Quartier Chraka.

To the salt works near Monastir; boat trips to the Kuriate islands about 20 km distant.

Ancient Towns.

In central Tunisia are some of the most important places to see in the country, including *Kairouan*, the religious capital of Tunisia, the ancient sites of *Maktar, Sufetula* (Sbeitla) and *El Djem*, and Mahdia, only 71 km from Sousse.

Mahdia Pop. 37,000

This town, situated on the promontory called the 'Cape of Africa', has attracted conquerors and pirates, and thus has a very varied history.

The old Phoenician port of *Gummi* became Romanised and then conquered by Obaid Allah, the first Fatimid ruler, who elevated the town to capital status (921–947). This Shiite prince, descended in a direct line from Fatima, the daughter of Mohammed, considered himself the *Mahdi*, the 'Warrior of faith, sent by God', and this gave the town its name.

Fortified Gate and Kasbah

Mahdia's modern fishing port is the largest and most important in Tunisia (other sources of income are olive cultivation, drilling for oil, wool and silk weaving). Behind the large covered fish market you come to the fortified gate, the *Skiffa El Khala*, erected in the 12th c. (with several later additions to its fortifications) as a monumental bastion against the interior.

Behind the fortified gate you come to the south bank and the *Great Mosque*, the first Fatimid mosque in Tunisia (912–921). Frequently altered, it was completely renovated between 1960 and 1965 in accordance with the original plans, thus regaining its old appearance.

If you go further east along the coast you come to the *Kasbah*, also called *Bordj El Kebir* (early 16th c.). In the middle of the 16th c. the Turkish corsair chieftain Dragut, who was feared throughout North Africa, had his headquarters here.

East of the Kasbah lies the ancient harbour; continuing in the same direction you reach the lighthouse and the remains of the town wall. If you return via Rue Mohammed Abdesselem, shortly before reaching the Great Mosque you pass the *Folklore Museum*, which is open to visitors. The picturesque streets make a stroll through the Old Town worth while.

Good sandy beaches. Initial steps have been taken to develop the town into a seaside resort.

El Djem

El Djem (French: El Jem)

42 km from Mahdia and 63 km from Sousse is a historic monument which you really must see; this massive *Roman Amphitheatre* is an incomparable sight towering over the flat desert in grandiose solitude, yet with the humble houses of a tiny village crowded nearby (from which both children and adults will come rushing with 'genuine Roman' souvenirs!).

Nobody knows exactly why, at the transition of the 2nd and 3rd centuries, the Proconsul Gordianus should have erected, in the comparatively unimportant place called *Thysdrus,* this huge building in which he himself was to be proclaimed emperor in his old age! Perhaps he needed an arena for the recently instituted persecution of the Christians and gladiatorial games, which could be held here before an audience of 35,000. Hundreds of lions and bears waited in their quarters to enter into the cruel spectacle, while up to 500 gladiators at a time presented the crowd with a scene of senseless, and mortal, combat. In the 7th c. the amphitheatre became a fortress, which the legendary Berber princess Kahena, an African 'Maid of Orleans', is said to have defended to the last against the Arab invaders.

In 1695, when more and more bands of robbers continued to use it as a hiding place, Mohammed Bey had a part of the building taken down, to make it easier for his soldiers to comb through it. Legend has a different explanation for its partial destruction: no scorpions could live within the walls of the amphitheatre, so later settlers incorporated stones from the old building into their houses, as amulets to drive away the poisonous stinging beasts.

148 m long, 122 m wide and 36 m high, the theatre of El Djem was the largest Roman amphitheatre in North Africa. Also worth seeing are the underground quarters for the animals, which were brought up to the arena by lift.

There is also a museum you can visit, with beautiful mosaics.

Kairouan Pop. 55,000

A good hour's journey from Sousse (68 km) transports you into another world. Kairouan is the Mecca of North Africa, the third holiest city of Islam.

Through an infertile steppe runs a well constructed road, across which whirl eddies of sand. The shabby houses of agricultural workers come into sight. Hedges of impenetrable fig-cactus protect them from sand-drifts, and at the same time provide safe pens for the small herds of sheep. From this seemingly endless steppe then appear the bright domes and minarets of the city, followed by the orange-brown of its walls. Neither Rome nor Carthage ever built here; it is purely Arab in character.

For the pious Muslim, seven pilgrimages to Kairouan are a substitute for one such journey to Mecca (except that they do not earn him the honorary

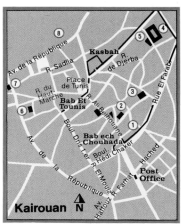

1 Zaouia Sidi Abid El Ghariani
2 Bir Barouta
3 Mosque of the Three Gates
4 Djamaa Sidi Okba
5 Museum
6 Sabre Mosque
7 Barber's Mosque
8 Pools of the Aghlabids

Great Mosque, Kairouan

title of a 'Hadj'). The holy waters of Mecca are said to be connected underground with the small Kairouan spring, the Bir Barouta, by which the horsemen of the Emir Okba Ben Nafi rested during his campaign of conquest in A.D. 671, when the great general decided to found a city here. This first purely Arab city became the arsenal of the Muslim conquerors, a trading centre where the caravan trains crossed, and a rich royal seat. After the ravaging nomadic hordes of Beni Hilal had razed it to the ground in 1057, Tunis did indeed become the political and spiritual centre, but Kairouan remained the bastion of Islam, the Holy City of North Africa.

📷 In the Medina

It is best to visit the city on a guided tour, or you can engage one of the officially authorised guides (many speak English) provided through the hotel or the tourist office (Syndicat d'Initiative). The latter is to be found in front of the *Bab ech-Chouhada*, the 'Martyrs' Gate', through which you enter the 900 m x 400 m Medina, and which also leads directly to the main street, Rue Ali Belhouane. If you visit the Medina without a guide, it is advisable to make enquiries at the tourist office regarding opening times and whether any entry passes are needed.

On the right behind the gate lies the *Zaouia Sidi Abid El Ghariani* (14th c.), the sepulchre of a saint, with a beautiful doorway and inner courtyard, and a magnificently decorated dome over the grave.

If you return to Rue Ali Belhouane and turn right at the next road junction into Rue des Cuirs, you will find the *Bir Barouta* (see above) in the upper storey of a pump room.

Going further in this direction, on the left-hand side of Rue de la Mosquée des Trois Portes you will come to the Mosque of the Three Gates (*Djamaa Tleta Bibane*), the ornamental façade of which (bands of script and bas-relief) dates from 866.

If you now strike out from here in a northerly direction, you will find in the north-east corner of the Medina the most important building in Tunisia, the Great Mosque named *Djamaa Sidi Okba*, after the founder of the city.

The first mosque on this site was built in 672, and formed at that time the centre of the city. The present-day building dates mainly from the 9th c. The Djamaa Sidi Okba is the first T-shaped mosque, and served as a pattern for the mosques built in the Maghreb.

In the inner courtyard, which is surrounded by pillars, can be seen an Arab sundial, and the flagstones of the yard cover a cistern. It is worth while climbing the 128 steps up to the 35-m-high imposing minaret, the architecture of which was modelled on the lighthouses of the time. From up there you will not only have a splendid view of the Medina, but you will also be able to appreciate the vast extent of the mosque grounds, which form a rectangle measuring 135 m x 80 m.

You cannot visit the prayer-hall of the mosque, which has 17 aisles and 414 columns of granite, porphyry and marble, and ancient and Byzantine capitals from all parts of the country. The showpiece in the prayer-hall is the

Kairouan Fantasia

Mihrab, the prayer-niche pointing towards Mecca and decorated in 862 with marble and golden faience tiles from Baghdad.

Finds worth seeing relating to the history of Kairouan and its Great Mosque are on display in the new 'Museum of Islamic Art' in Raggada, 12 km from Kairouan.

Outside the city walls

You leave the Medina in the north through the Tunis Gate (*Bab Et Tounis*), in front of which lies the busy Place de Tunis. Turning left into Rue de Haut Marché, you come upon the *Sabre Mosque* (Zaouia Sidi Amor Abbada), which certainly looks medieval, but in fact dates from the 19th c. It is the mausoleum of a swordsmith before whom the Holy Ghost appeared, after which he made only enormous sabres, and had this dazzlingly white domed building erected as a memorial. Continuing in a north-westerly direction, you arrive at the *Barber's Mosque* (Zaouia Sidi Sahab), on the Avenue de la République; it has little to do with a barber, however. The holy Sahab, when present once at the shaving of Mohammed, kept three hairs from the beard of the prophet for himself, and carried them with him until he died. The Zaouia was later built over his 7th c. grave and was frequently altered, the last time in the 19th c. Nevertheless, the building still displays a special architectural grace

In the streets of Kairouan

Pools of the Aghlabids, Kairouan

in the elegance of its colonnades and the particularly beautiful Tunisian faience tiles covering the walls. Further along the Avenue de la République you will find the *Pools of the Aghlabids*, constructed in 862. The large 48-sided water basin is 128 m in diameter, and the ruler's pavilion once stood on the platform in the middle. The small pool, 37 m in diameter, served as a purification pool. The basin was supplied with water from the hills via a 36-km-long aqueduct.

The Souks

You should give yourself time to visit the streets and souks after seeing the famous buildings. If possible, book a trip which stops overnight in Kairouan. The nightlife, a cup of tea in a Moorish café, and a visit to a carpet dealer (there are 1500 carpet makers in the city) will round off the picture nicely for you. Do not let the fact that your guide will keep pressing carpets on you lead you into making an impulsive purchase — he is probably on commission! However, you actually can buy original and good carpets in Kairouan. Do look out for the official seal of quality (see page 22).

Maktar Pop. 7000

115 km from Kairouan, the Roman *Marctaris* was built on a Punic settlement. Like Thuburbo Majus, it reached its peak in the 2nd c., becoming rich as a trans-shipment centre for oil, corn and cattle.

A walk around Maktar

Coming from the present-day Maktar, you enter the ruined town through the Roman gate, the *Gate of Springs* (Bab El Ain), where the Punic sacrificial site, the Tophet (see page 38), used to be. There are gravestones and urns in the small museum opposite the Gate of Springs. Behind the museum, near the road leading into the area of the ruins, are the remains of the *Amphitheatre*. 250 m further on you come to the former Forum and, on its south side, the *Triumphal Arch of Trajan*, dating from the year 116. The inscription extols Trajan as the greatest of all rulers. Further to the south are the foundations of the *Basilica of Hildegundus* (5th c.) and, after about 100 m, the *Great Baths*, the best-preserved Roman thermal baths in Africa. Beautifully kept floor mosaics

(A.D. 200) can still be seen between the 12–15-m-high walls, especially in the Frigidarium.

If you take the road branching off to the west you will arrive at the second great site in Maktar, the *Schola Juvenum* (School of Young People). Here the young men of well-to-do families received not only a higher education, but also schooling in political and military skills. Even during their period of education they performed a certain military function; they were put under the control of the magistrate and employed in supporting the military. This form of institution was found in a number of Roman towns sited near the frontiers. You can still see remains of the colonnade around the *Palaestra* (gymnasium), once a large building, and of the lecture rooms and assembly halls; there are also gravestones, because it was later used as a church.

Gate of Antoninus Pius, Sbeitla

1 Triumphal Arch of Diocletian
2-4 Remains of Byzantine fortifications
5 Church
6 Winter baths
7 Theatre
8 Servas Church
9 Forum
10 Gate of Antoninus Pius
11 Capitol Temples
12 Church of Bellator Jucundus Chapel Vitalis Church
13 Temple
14 Villa
15 Church
16 Bridge

On returning north towards the entrance, you will come to the *Numidian Market* opposite the ruins of a *Temple to Bacchus*. To the north-west are the rather unimpressive remains of the *North Baths*.

Somewhere in the Maktar region — historians dispute the exact site — the famous battle of Zama was fought in which Hannibal, the Carthaginian general, was finally defeated by the Romans and had to leave North Africa for ever (202 B.C.).

Sbeitla Pop. 12,000; Alt. 537 m

Most circular tours of Tunisia will make a stop at Sbeitla, 107 km south-west of Kairouan, because there, in the middle of the barren semi-desert landscape, parts of the old Roman town of *Sufetula* still remain. Sufetula, in the 7th c. a Byzantine stronghold and the seat of the Byzantine Exarch Gregory, was destroyed during the first Arab invasion in 647, and only saved from oblivion by French archaeologists at the beginning of this century. The somewhat monotonous journey to Sbeitla is rewarded by encountering a ruined town

Entrance to the Medina, Sfax

of impressive size, about 1200 m long and 500 m wide.

A walk around Sbeitla

The moment you arrive here from Kairouan you will spy the well preserved *Triumphal Arch of Diocletian*, once the south gate of the town. Behind the present-day entrance you will first of all come across remains of *Byzantine fortifications*, and nearby the outline of a church can still be discerned. Then follow the *Winter Baths* and, below them by the river, the small *Theatre*.

Past the foundation walls of the 5th c. *Servas Church* lies the *Forum*, measuring 60 m x 70 m and surrounded by a 4-m-high wall with restored columns. It is entered through the still imposing triple-arched *Gate of Antoninus Pius* (A.D. 139). Opposite the gate stand the three *Capitol Temples* dedicated to Juno (left), Jupiter (centre) and Minerva (right). Further north from the Forum are remains of the *Diocesan Church of Bellator*, the *Jucundus Chapel* and the *Vitalis Church* (left) with a lovely mosaic font.

In the north-west of the grounds the sparse remains of a temple, a villa and another church can still be seen. Going directly north from here you will come to the river, spanned by a bridge built on the foundations of an aqueduct.

Sfax Pop. 232,000

This, the largest town after Tunis, lies in one of the most well-to-do regions of the country. It is a nerve centre controlling the trade and economy of the south, situated where the great cross-country roads from the Sahel converge. Oil presses and tenders stand ready to deal with the harvest from the seven million olive trees which account for the wealth of the area. Each year 70,000 tonnes of alfa grass are sent overseas from here, and 200,000 tonnes of phosphate are transported from the mines of Gafsa province. The fact that the town is also a fishery centre brings a totally different colour into its life; in the harbour hundreds of fishing boats come and go, including the brightly decorated craft of the sponge fishers, who like the other fishermen auction off their catch at the harbour itself.

 Sfax grew up on the site of the ancient *Taparura*, from the stones of which the Kasbah and the mosques were built. The town wall, dating from the 9th c., and the Great Mosque (restored in the 18th c.) remind us of the glittering epoch of the Aghlabid rulers. Economic development began a century later; at that time Sfax already exported olive oil and was famed as a supplier of a special milled cloth. During the middle of the 12th c. Sfax, like the rest of the coast, experienced some years of domination by Normans who came from Sicily.

In the last war Sfax suffered heavy damage from air-raids and the rebuilding has changed the face of the town.

 The *New Town*, between the port and Avenue Habib Bourguiba, which starts at the railway station, has been rebuilt in a modern style. Here you will find streets and squares shaded by palm trees, and attractive restaurants, with cuttlefish of all kinds figuring prominently on the menu.

At the Place de la République the Avenue Habib Bourguiba is crossed by the magnificent Avenue Hedi Chaker which runs from the harbour to the Medina. At the junction stands the *Town Hall* which houses a small museum.

The Avenue Hedi Chaker leads in a northerly direction to the monumental Medina gate, the *Bab Divan*, erected in 1346 and restored after the war. Behind it lies the very colourful Medina. Everywhere you will encounter decoratively sculptured doors and gates, the stone embellishment of which displays a typically Sfax style. You will come across some beautiful courtyards and attractive houses which you can enter if you are accompanied by a guide.

In the centre of the Medina stands the *Great Mosque*, which was begun in 849 but which has been enlarged over the centuries in successive new styles.

East of the mosque is a craft museum (*Musée des Arts et des Traditions Populaires*), housed in an 18th c. palace with a beautiful courtyard, the *Dar Djellouli*.

 About 25 km to the bathing beach of *Plage Chaffar*, a holiday resort with villas in the Moorish style.

 Novotel Syphax.

 Le Corail, 39 Av. Habib Maazoun; *Le Printemps*, 57 Avenue Habib Bourguiba; *Le Chandelier*, Rue Alex. Dumas.

 Office de Tourisme, Place de l'Indépendance.

Kerkennah Islands

20 km off the coast from Sfax lie the Kerkennah Islands; the sea here is shallow and full of sandbanks, so it has been possible to link the two main islands of Gharbi and Chergui with a causeway.

The islands barely rise out of the sea and are quite flat. Apart from the tourist trade the principal source of income for the 15,000 inhabitants is fishing, in part still employing traditional techniques. The V-shaped posts in the shallow waters are fish-traps, just like those used in olden times.

Famous throughout Tunisia is Kerkennah sauce, made from tomatoes and a lot of garlic and excellent with crayfish, shrimps and prawns.

Kerkennah's traditional folk dances are among the best-preserved in the country. These islands offer the visitor a choice of both luxury and unusual hotels.

By horse or donkey.

Sfax-Gharbi three times daily; crossing takes at least one hour.

Oasis of Gabès

The Gulf of Gabès

The further south you come from Sfax, the more the countryside loses its green appearance, to be replaced by the greyish-yellow of the steppe and desert.

There are now scarcely any more museums and archaeological sites to visit; the sights to be seen in the south stem from the unique characteristics of the landscape, and demonstrate the ways in which human life has developed there. They possess the great charm of the exotic and — the further south you go — of the wholly un-European.

One of the three tourist centres on the Gulf of Gabès, which in days gone by was called 'Little Syrthe', is Gabès itself, an oasis situated right by the sea. For those who are keen on exploring and would like to see as much of the country as possible, Gabès makes an ideal starting point; there are good roads and bus routes in all directions, and rail-cars go to Sfax (about 2 hours) and Tunis.

The visitor who is not looking for organised entertainment, but who nevertheless would like to make excursions to places of interest, is well catered for in the holiday centres on the Gulf of Gabès. From Djerba, the largest of all the North African islands, from Zarzis, with its many sporting facilities, and from Gabès itself there are tours into the interior lasting one or more days.

Gabès Pop. 93,000 approx.
This interesting seaside resort lies 138 km south of Sfax. It was originally a

Phoenician trading post. After the fall of Carthage, the Numidian king Massinissa seized this port and helped the

Romans to incorporate it into their empire, as the colony of *Tacapae*.

 Sightseeing

Gabès, which lost a little of its character as a result of rebuilding following war damage in 1942, and destruction by the storms of 1962, extends along the south bank of the river of the same name, which the oasis has to thank for its development. There, where the little river enters the sea, lies the town harbour. To the south begins the holiday and beach zone.

The main commercial street is Avenue Président Habib Bourguiba, which sweeps round near the river. Here is the centre of the town, with the *Great Mosque* (built in 1952), the market place and the picturesque alleyways of the old Arab quarter *Grand Djara*. Near the mausoleum of Sidi Bou Lbaba a *museum* provides information on the history and traditions of the region. Behind the new market hall is a carpet-making school which you can visit.

On the far side of the river lies *Petit Djara*, an Arab quarter also worth seeing. The five to six kilometres of date groves around the oasis enclose two further Arab quarters. The oasis forms a confusing labyrinth of green paths, steep hills and dense fruit gardens. It would take hours to wander through them, and finding your way back alone — for the first time at least — would be pretty hopeless. Unfortunately, however, most guided tours are too short and all too often the guide spares himself the climb to the points with the best views. If you hire a horse-drawn cart, haggle over the price before you get in.

 Flat beaches of fine sand with deck-chairs and sunshades.

     At the beach.

 Rowing and motorboats at the harbour.

Matmata

 Giant prawns *(crevettes royales)* and best quality dates *(deglet nour)* in various restaurants.

 Saharan dress: embroidered shoes, trousers and ladies' blouses, and Berber jewellery.

 Matmata Alt. 400 m

You will get a foretaste of a desert trip by joining an excursion to Matmata on the Saharan plateau which begins 43 km south of Gabès. Matmata lies in a rather desolate plain surrounded by hills. No houses are to be seen in the furrowed yellow-brown hills; at one time Berber tribes, forced into this harsh mountainous land by the invading Arabs, proved themselves to be excellent cave architects. Giant shafts, with wells at the bottom, are connected by long tunnels with living rooms, stables, provision stores and kitchens — veritable underground houses, some of which are still lived in today. There is even a cave hotel!

On Djerba

The Island of Djerba

Djerba, covering an area of some 400 sq. km, is a flat, truly African island, characterised by oases, many date-palms, wide areas of sand and beaches and 3770 wells. The saying goes that once upon a time a good fairy conjured a complete oasis out of the Sahara into the Mediterranean in order to create a paradise on earth, and it was in this paradise that Odysseus, returning from the Trojan War, forgot to continue his journey home. Djerba is said to have been the island of the mysterious 'lotus eaters', the *Lotophagi*. The lotus, an almost translucent fruit which some suspect might have been the date, tasted so delicious that anyone who ate of it never wanted to leave the island. Even today the island, with its two million date-palms and half a million olive trees, works a mysterious magic on many foreigners who, following the spirit of the times, buy flats of their own here or even build villas.

Djerba measures 28 km from east to west and 22 km from north to south. A total of 92,000 people live on the island, but they are no longer dependent on its wells; the springs in Djebel Dahar in the south of Médenine have been tapped and the island is provided with fresh water by means of a huge pipe system. You need not worry therefore about being able to take a shower, but this 'spring water' should be boiled before drinking.

If you travel to Djerba by air, you will land at the international airport of *Mellita*, which belongs to the island's little capital town of *Houmt Souk*. However, Djerba is also easy to reach from the mainland; the northern part of the island is connected by regular ferries (also for coaches and cars) from Adjim to Djorf on the mainland, and from the southern tip of the island a solid causeway, originating from Roman times, leads to the African continent. Both ends of the causeway are named *El Kantara* (the bridge).

An eventful past

The island, called *Meninx* in ancient times and famous then for the dye from

Market, Djerba

its purple snails, has had, like the rest of the coast, a somewhat eventful history.

Under the Carthaginians, who incidentally introduced the olive tree, and the Romans the island of Djerba was a busy port used for both military and mercantile purposes, developing an extensive trade in slaves, ivory, amber, gold and animal hides. To make it easier for the caravans to transport these African goods, the Romans built the causeway to the mainland.

On this island, too, Vandals, Byzantines, Normans, Spaniards and Arabs carried on their power struggles, until the Spaniards finally established themselves here in the 16th c. This was much against the will of the people, however, and the Djerbis constantly used to hide near the vital wells and lure the Spaniards there to trap them. In 1560 the whole Spanish garrison of Djerba met a terrible end: the corsair chief, Dragut, seized the island with the help of a Turkish fleet, sank the Spanish ships sent to relieve it, and had the whole Christian garrison of 5,000 men slaughtered. From the skulls of the dead

the Turks erected a victory monument in the form of a pyramid which, under the name of *Bordj-Er-Ras* (Tower of Skulls), remained standing until 1848. Then the Bey had the tower taken down and the bones given a Christian burial.

Apart from the capital town of *Houmt Souk*, Djerba has only village settlements, often very remote, with pretty domed houses and mosques.

The Djerbis

The inhabitants of Djerba, the Djerbis, are a special breed of people who have retained much that is pure Berber in their speech, dress and customs. The oldest Berber dialect is spoken here; Muslims who abide by the rare and puritanical code of the *Kharedjits* are in the majority, and both men and women wear traditional costume (varying slightly from place to place), which gives the whole picture its colour.

A large Jewish community of some 4000 lives on Djerba in close contact with its Muslim neighbours but strictly in accordance with its own religious rules. You really must visit the villages of *Hara*

La Ghriba Synagogue Hostel, Djerba

Srira and *Hara Kebira* (Hara means 'bitter').

A holiday on Djerba

On Djerba everything is relatively peaceful. The island is large and quiet with small markets to stroll around and friendly people who leave you in peace. The mild climate does a lot to help you to relax. It is certainly not assumed that you will want to leap into the sea in winter time when the water temperature is about 13°C, but perhaps when you are tired you may care to go swimming in a heated swimming pool? Do not let the wind worry you; even in summer, and especially in the evenings, it can blow quite strongly over the island.

Discothèques and dances provide your evening entertainment, as do appearances by folk troupes and orchestras in the hotels. Outstanding too are the *Gougous* who perform here, a black troupe whose ancestors were brought here as slaves from the Sudan. Their warlike dances are extremely dramatic.

Houmt Souk Pop. 34,000

The capital of the island is delightfully situated on the north coast, but should only be considered as a holiday base by those seeking the charm of the surroundings and not principally interested in bathing.

An avenue of eucalyptus trees follows the line of the coast as far as the old Spanish fortress *Bordj Elkébir* which, although dating probably from the 13th—14th c., has been frequently altered, and which today, with its café

Mosque, Djerba

and lovely view, is a favourite spot for tourists out walking. Between the fort and the harbour stands the memorial to the *Tower of Skulls* (see page 75).

The delicately rounded minaret of the *Djamaa Trouk* reveals it from afar as a 'Turkish mosque'. You should also not fail to see the *Djamaa Ghorba*, the foreign mosque, and also the *Zaouia Sidi Brahim El Djamni* which dates from the 17th—18th c.

The prettiest route of all is a stroll through the souks, by way of the square with its Moorish café and the market which is held on Mondays and Thursdays. Many of the tiny shops have given way to newer communal stalls belonging to the 'Syndicates'. But the goldsmiths still sell little boxes containing Bedouin jewellery, pretty chains and necklaces.

Worth seeing is the fish auction held in the market hall.

The sea here is not suitable for bathing. You will have to take the bus (the return journey costs about 30p) to the nearest and uniquely beautiful beaches at *Sidi Mahrez* (11 km). Depending upon internal agreements it is usually possible to use the beach of a corresponding hotel.

Harouan by the harbour: fish specialities; *Ettebsi*, as you enter the town: Tunisian specialities.

Connected with a big folk festival in August, a traditional wedding for tourists to watch is arranged in Houmt Souk.

At the *Office de l'Artisanat* you can obtain information on prices.

At the end of August there is a wind-surfing regatta in Houmt Souk.

Djerba's beaches

Djerba's bathing-beaches all lie on the eastern side of the island. As recently as 1960 they were worthless dunes. Since then more than 20 km of wild dunes have been converted into well cared for hotel gardens with pavilions and swimming pools, swings and sunshades. The beaches, with no villages but only hotels, were given names such as *Sidi Mahrez*. You can walk for hours along these beaches and still find quiet and secluded spots. Fine light-coloured sand, which is virtually flat as it meets the sea, delights the modern water-nomad. The only small hill on the island, which otherwise is 'as flat as an Arab loaf', is near the lighthouse in *Cap Tourgueness*. The wide beaches, with small rocky coves here and there, are a diver's paradise.

Near the cape is the largest hotel complex at present on the island, *Dar Djerba*, a holiday town with 2500 beds as

well as restaurants, boutiques, night clubs, casinos and sports facilities. At the same time there are plenty of quiet and secluded spots to be found in the extensive grounds.

On the beaches, where hotel life and bathing are concentrated, you will find plenty of opportunities for sporting activities.

At Cap Tourgueness and also along the rest of the coast, since the island lies on a rocky base beginning at a depth of 7–8 m.

In the vicinity of the *Club Méditerranée* (on the east side of the island) you can often find some of the sponge-fishers' barques, known as *loudes*; you are certain to find some in the height of summer in the fishing village of *Adjim* (see page 81) on the south-west coast. These are some of the few typical Arab boats in the Mediterranean which still carry the triangular lateen sail on a tall pliable mast. Their number is getting smaller, but to go out in such a boat is a most unusual experience; one of the fishermen watches the water below the surface through a kind of box-mirror, while a diver, acting on his instructions, spears sponges or fish with a harpoon. In Adjim the Maître de Port (harbour-master) can arrange for a boat to take you out during the period of the great mérou catch in high summer. The mérou is a perch-like fish up to 1.5 m long.

      Paddle boats.

     On the beach; horses, donkeys and camels.

At almost all hotels, including thermal swimming-baths — warning: your swimming costume may possibly turn brown!

    Hotels have their own courts but not always of the standard

common in Europe. *Tennishotel Méditerranée*: 12 courts, floodlighting, tennis coaching.

 At numerous hotels.

 Also motor-scooters.

 A tour of the island.

As well as joining excursions to the mainland you can make a circular tour of the island by bus or go exploring on a bicycle.

Hara Kebira Pop. 1000: 2 km from Houmt Souk lies the Jewish village where you can eat the best *briks* cooked in oil (see page 21). Also there are attractive embroidered articles for sale.

Hara Srira Pop. 3000: This is where the largest part of the Jewish community lives. The men's dress scarcely differs from that of the Muslims. The women, on the other hand, have pretty embroidered caps, the specially decorated centre-piece of which peeps out of the shawl thrown over the head.

To the south of the village stands the famous pilgrimage synagogue of *La Ghriba*, which means 'wonderful' or rather 'strange' in Arabic. A holy stone from heaven is said to have fallen here — a stone from the destroyed temple in Jerusalem. As a building, the synagogue is nothing special. In its present form it dates from the turn of the century. In the interior, however, which men can enter only if their heads are covered, you are transported into a strange, Old Testament atmosphere. The most important treasures to be seen in the synagogue are old Thora rolls and ritual objects. In May the synagogue is the destination of pilgrims from the whole of North Africa and France, and in the autumn it is the scene of the Yom-Kippur festival.

Sedouikech: You should visit this large village, which has a market on Tuesdays, in order to see the pointed straw hats, the *petases*, handed down from ancient Greek times, which the women wear over their white veils.

Guelalla, Djerba

Guelalla (23 km): Hills of clay-marl provide the raw materials for the potters whose work you will see from afar, set out on the hillsides to dry. The colourful village square is charming.

Midoun Pop. 18,000: Situated in the east of the island this, the largest place after Houmt Souk, provides an unusually colourful picture on market day, Friday. Very striking are the typical large straw hats worn by the men. The main square with its bars and Moorish cafés, bright mosques and beautiful gardens is most attractive. If you have an appetite for grasshoppers you can buy them in the market.

Mahboubine: In its 19th c. *El Kateb Mosque*, set in the midst of rich olive groves and fruit plantations, the village possesses the most beautiful mosque in Djerba, which somewhat resembles in miniature the world-famous Hagia Sophia in Istanbul.

El Kantara: Near this village on the island you can find relics from Roman times, and some 4 km away ruins of the ancient port of *Meninx*.

Houmt Souk, Djerba

On the beach at Zarzis

Adjim: 21 km (good road) from Houmt Souk, this village is not only interesting for those taking part in the mérou fishing (see page 78), for here the sponge fishers offer the proceeds of their dangerous work for sale on the sponge market.

Zarzis Pop. 50,000

27 km from the island of Djerba lies Zarzis, to date the most southerly holiday resort on the Tunisian coast. The township itself, which grew up in the 19th c., offers little — a small French fort and a picturesque harbour, given colour by the barques of the sponge fishers. Friday is the chief market day. Artesian wells near the town enable palm forests to flourish, in the shade of which nestle small villages, together with a seemingly endless beach. Here, amidst well tended gardens, stand the hotels, an hour's walk from Zarzis.

A walk into the low hills changes the picture: camel and donkey drivers, and women going to the well with water-jugs on their heads, create a colourful oriental backdrop.

 The degree of quiet depends on the situation of the hotel; being too near to the discothèque or the folk-music platform may shorten your night's sleep!

At the hotels.

 Horses, donkeys and camels on the beach.

 Paddle-boats.

 Freshwater or thermal pools at the hotels.

 At several hotels.

 In the hotels.

 Sahara roses (rosette-shaped stones) in all sizes.

In June *Festival de l'Eponge*, the festival of the sponge fishers.

The Desert

After the lush green strips of vegetation in the north and the adjoining Sahel zone, the third type of landscape in Tunisia is the desert.

The vast expanse of sand-dunes, the encrusted surfaces of the chotts (salt lakes), the dark mountain ranges — all combine to produce scenes of oppressive solitude. In the midst of this barren waste the springs of the oases serve to bring colour to the life of the region. *Bled el Djerid* (land of palms), or Djerid for short, is the name given to the area which extends as far as the northern shores of the *El Djerid* Chott. Here lie the great Djerid oases. At each of these fortunate spots the water-sources provide nourishment for several hundreds of thousands of date-palms. The *deglet nour* (sun date) is famous for its size and sweetness; the best quality is mainly reserved for export. The date harvest in December is usually the occasion of a great festival. Nowadays in the oases a 'three-storeyed' form of cultivation is practised: in the shade of the giant palms grow fruit trees and beneath them vegetables are planted.

Nomads

While the Sahel had since time immemorial been the land of farming settlers, the interior belonged to the nomads. With their herds of camels, donkeys, goats and sheep they were constantly on the move in search of food, and they put up their squat tents sometimes in the uplands of the west and sometimes near the oases in Djerid. The nomads have become fewer, but you still occasionally encounter them with their camel-herds and their strange black tents, the occupants of which do not usually appreciate visitors.

Desert dwellings

The Chott El Djerid, a 150-km-long dried-up salt lake, narrows to a point as it runs towards the coast. It forms a definite boundary between the zones. On its south side begins the Sahara, through which run Tunisia's frontiers with Algeria and Libya. West of Médenine the Sahara plateau emerges, determining the face of this landscape; men have for centuries adapted their mode of living to suit its conditions. In the Matmata region to the north (see page 73) they dug whole cave-villages out of the hillsides — troglodyte dwellings which afford protection against the sudden changes in temperature. In the Médenine region, on the other hand, they have built the *ghorfas*, honey-

comb-like rooms arranged one against the other, with barrel-vaulted roofs, which are accessible only by external staircases, and which can be used as storage rooms to protect food stocks from wind, dust and sun, while also serving as refuges for the nomads. A network of asphalt roads from the coastal towns is extending further and further into the desert. The oases *Tozeur* and *Nefta*, as well as *Kebili* and *Douz*, can now easily be reached by car. In the much visited oases you will find comfortable accommodation, inviting you to stay longer.

Médenine Alt. 104 m; Pop. 26,000

Here, 35 km from Zarzis, you will come across the first *ghorfas*. This fortress-like complex, near which remains of an old fortified provision store are preserved, is called *Ksar* (fort) here. The defensive parts of the ghorfas, which themselves are no longer used today, were removed during the Protectorate period as a precaution against possible pockets of resistance. So today you get only a faint idea of how secure these vaulted buildings once were against attack.

🚌 A trip into the hilly region of Dahar takes you via Beni Kheddache (36 km) up into the lonely *Ksar Djouama*, some 500 m high (about a further 25 km). As soon as you arrive you will see the ghorfas built round a hill on your left. Today the place is deserted and you can wander quite peacefully through the dilapidated ghorfas.

From Médenine an asphalt road leads south to *Foum Tatahouine*, which is surrounded by inhabited and uninhabited ghorfa settlements. 130 km on from Foum Tatahouine, at *Ramada*, the asphalt road becomes a desert track.

Ksar Haddad

The main things to note on the single-storey ghorfas at Ksar Haddad (30 km from Foum Tatahouine) are the Berber and Arabic inscriptions at the entrances.

Excursion in the desert

Ksar Haddad

 The Ksar Haddad *Cave Hotel* provides a very special experience.

Chenini Pop. 1500

A unique Berber village, situated far to the south (16 km from Ksar Haddad, 10 km from Foum Tatahouine), the houses of which are set deep in the rock. You will have to do quite a lot of climbing and you should wear stout shoes on the steep and winding path up to the ridge. There is a splendid view from the square of the *Mosque on the Hill*. Ask here for the Underground Mosque (*Mosquée souterraine*), near the cemetery. According to legend this is the place where the 'seven sleepers' lay hidden, but there are about a dozen places in the Mediterranean which make the same claim. The legendary seven sleepers of Ephesus were young men who took refuge in a cave to evade religious persecution. They were walled up and slept for one hundred years.

 Spend the night in a Berber tent in the *Campement Berbère*.

Douirat Pop. 1000

This place — very near Chenini — is not yet widely advertised to desert travellers. Here too you will find dwellings formed in the soft rock. The old part is dominated by a kind of fortress which was a corn store and hiding-place. The caravan trail from Ghadames to Gabès passes here.

Ksar Rhilane

It is scarcely 60 km as the crow flies from Douirat to Ksar Rhilane, but what an adventure it is to travel for hours through desolate desert country. The scarcely discernible roads are swept by treacherous drifting sand; ridges in the sand, conjured up by the gentle breeze and looking like vehicle tracks, lead the unwary astray. You must never travel alone, only in convoy. It is also best to inform the nearest Tunisian police post.

Ksar Rhilane is an old outpost for the camel riders of the French Foreign Legion. Here they erected their boundary mark, the *Monument of the Leclerc Company*.

The track now leads further northwards, in part along the oil pipeline which runs from the El Borma oilfield and is operated jointly by Tunisia and Algeria, to the El Skhira oil depot north of Gabès.

Kebili

This oasis on the edge of the Chott El Djerid, with some 800,000 date-palms, is an administrative centre.

Drivers and desert travellers, whether in a jeep or on a dromedary, come first of all to the *Ras El Ain*, the famous spring of Kebili (in the direction of Douz). Here you can leap into the pool and enjoy a refreshing bathe with the young people of the village. The spring-water runs through the oasis in numerous small brooks, providing adequate irrigation for the fruit and vegetable gardens. It is worth while climbing up to the minaret of one of the old mosques.

Negro slaves, brought from the Sudan by caravans, were still being traded in Kebili up to the middle of the last century.

Ghorfas (wheat stores),
Ksar Haddad

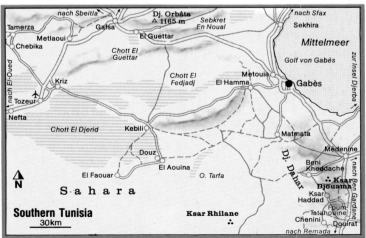

The dark-skinned inhabitants of the oasis are descendants of these slaves.

 At the beginning of this century, when ostrich feathers were very much sought after, there was an ostrich farm here. The Hotel *Borj des Autruches* (Ostrich Castle) reminds us of that.

In Kebili and on the road to Douz there is a plentiful supply of sand-roses at favourable prices. These bizarre crystalline creations, rose-like but up to a metre across, are derived from sulphate deposits which occur in the desert soil.

Douz Pop. 16,000 (Region)

Douz, like Kebili, is one of those small oases to which excursions are often made in the course of a cross-country journey. Bedouins come from afar to the market on Thursdays. In the last week of December the Sahara Festival presents an unusual spectacle (camel-races, dancing, games on horseback). Here you will find beautiful 'desert subjects' for your camera and, with luck, you may even snap some of the men with the blue cloaks, Tuaregs, who often camp nearby.

Office de Tourisme, Place de la République.

The Chott El Djerid

On the 100-km road, partially asphalted, which connects Kebili with Tozeur, crossing the great salt lake of Chott El

Berber village of Chenini in southern Tunisia

Djerid is no longer a problem. Leaving the road, however, can be highly dangerous.

The salt lake is well known for its mirages. Oases appear on the horizon and disappear again. Nobody can say in advance when and where such a 'Fata Morgana' will appear. The rule-of-thumb guide says the hotter it is, the more Fata Morganas. In the countryside surrounding Chott El Djerid good quality water is brought to the surface from a depth of 2000 m. This enables the desert landscape to be converted into an agrarian zone.

🚐 'Sailing-car parties' across the Chott El Djerid can be booked in the Hotel *El Djerid* in Tozeur.

Tozeur Pop. 21,000

The town will surprise you with the unique ornamentation on its houses. Geometrically arranged bricks provide the façades with carpet-like patterns. Especially pretty houses and a small museum are to be found in the oldest quarter *Ouled Hadef*, east of the main street, Avenue Habib Bourguiba. The Ibn Chabbath square, with its market place and post office, forms the town centre.

The Oasis of Tozeur adjoins the town in the east and south. It is one of the largest and perhaps one of the most beautiful oases in Tunisia. Two hundred springs, which come together into a river and send out a network of small tributaries, irrigate the oasis.

You will get a good impression of the place if you ride on the back of a dromedary to *Paradise*, some 3 km south of the town. You reach it by way of *Bled El Hader*, with its 11th c. mosque and the domed tomb of Sidi Ali Bou Lifa, near which stands a giant jujube tree (*Le grand Jujubier*). Passing through a date-grove you finally arrive at Paradise, a 'Garden of Eden' rich in flowers and fruit.

About the same distance away is *Belvédère*, a group of rocks towering over the oasis, which offers a magnificent view.

North of the town is a desert zoo, with lions, desert-foxes, gazelles, jackals, black scorpions, etc. The snake and lizard demonstrations presented by the zoo owner Si Tijani are known throughout Tunisia. A further tip: Tozeur is the centre of the mysterious *Teggaza*, the soothsayers and clairvoyants. Their predictions regarding world catastrophes, royal weddings and political events are published in all Tunisian newspapers at the beginning of the year. Your hotel reception will certainly arrange for you to see a Teggaza who speaks French, and you can also bring an interpreter with you. Of course, a genuine Teggaza will also know the contents of your wallet — and will demand a 'suitable' fee!

✈ Tunis, Gabès.

🛏 Hotel *Oasis, Continental, Les Villas du Club*.

🎷 Musical event *The Purification of the Spring* in May; *Oasis Festival* in December.

ℹ *Office de Tourisme*, Av. Aboul Kacem-El Chabbi.

Oasis of Tozeur

Tips for desert travellers

The adventure really begins where the asphalt road ends. A Land Rover is the ideal vehicle. When the asphalt roads peter out you should make enquiries at the gendarmerie posts regarding the nature and suitability of the tracks. A sand-track which initially is quite good for driving on will often suddenly change to a stony, bumpy path; holes filled by drifting sand can result in a fatal crash.

When you stop for a rest, do not just sit down at random on a stone. You could disturb a scorpion or snake dozing underneath. Be careful, too, if you take your shoes off — the shady interior will prove an attractive refuge for scorpions! So make sure you shake your shoes thoroughly before putting them on again, and the same goes for jackets and any other items of clothing.

The lizards, like armadillos with scaly tails, are harmless; they are happiest if left undisturbed. They are a protected species! Time and again at the oases you will be offered stuffed lizards, but the British customs may well confiscate these macabre souvenirs. On the other hand, you will have no problems if you take through Sahara-roses, objects made from desert sand or crystals.

You will cause a lot of trouble if you try to peer into the wickerwork shelters which house the womenfolk on the dromedaries of a passing Bedouin family. One of the 'ships of the desert' always carries one of these baskets, almost as tall as a man and hung with brightly coloured fabrics, in which sit the female members of the family. The women can see out quite well through the fine mesh curtains, but those outside cannot see in.

Nefta Pop. 15,000 (Region)

23 km by bus from Tozeur, and only 36 km from the Algerian border, lies Nefta, a typical Saharan oasis and — like Tozeur

— often described as the most beautiful in Tunisia. Nefta is at the same time the religious centre of the Djerid, with 12 mosques and over 100 marabouts.

The town lies to the right and left of a deep, lush, green gorge named *La Corbeille* (the basket), through which the river flows. A bridge connects the two sections of the town.

Coming from Tozeur, you arrive first in the eastern part with its market, colourful souks and the dam and distribution system for the irrigation of the oasis.

On the other side of the gorge lies the still older part of the town. In the winding alleys you will come across many mosques and marabouts. There is a lovely view from the *Café de la Corbeille* in the north of the town.

The actual oasis, fed by 150 springs, begins on the southern edge of the town and extends as far as the Chott El Djerid. In the centre of the huge oasis lies a much visited destination for pilgrims, the Marabout of Sidi Bou Ali, a Moroccan saint who lived in the 13th c.

 Luxury hotel *Sahara Palace*.

 In the Café de la Corbeille; by request in the Sahara Palace.

 Folk Festival in April (parades and camel contests).

Chabika

This oasis lies 65 km north-west of Tozeur. You get to it by a good track which is already partly asphalted. Here you are in the Algerian border zone; military patrols and police check-points are frequently seen. Chabika was a Roman fortress and kept a watch on the caravan trail to Gabès. Worth seeing are the springs rising out of the red-brown rocks. A small waterfall in the midst of the lush vegetation makes you forget the nearby desert.

Tamerza Alt. 700 m

Up a narrow stony path lies Tamerza, the

most beautiful mountain oasis in Tunisia, the history of which goes back to Roman times. In the Byzantine epoch it was the see of a bishop. The tired and dust-covered traveller will do well to ask first for the swimming pool (*piscine*) and then for the waterfalls (*cascades*) which are well worth seeing.

You will frequently come across deserted settlements; the former inhabitants have gone to seek their fortune in the coastal towns or mining areas. Modern deep borings in the mountains are seeking water not oil.

Metlaoui Pop. 30,000
This small industrial town is the main handling centre for the phosphates mined in the area. The state *Compagnie des Phosphates* has its head office here. It employs 8000 men and has its own 'phosphate railway' which runs as far as the loading harbour of Sfax. The quarry area can be visited. There is a small museum in the town with a fossil collection.

Gafsa Pop. 61,000; Alt. 350 m
42 km from Metlaoui and 150 km from Gabès lies the provincial capital of Gafsa on the Ouëd Baiech, which quickly overflows its banks when rain falls. Gafsa is not a particularly characteristic oasis.

The *Kasbah*, standing on Byzantine foundations, has been frequently rebuilt. It was destroyed in 1943 following the explosion of a German munitions store, and rebuilt after the war. The main feature dates from the days of the Romans when the town was named *Caspa*. Two deep 'Roman swimming baths' (*Piscines romaines*), built with square stone blocks and supplied by a hot spring at 25°, form a genuine attraction in the centre of the town. Boys of all sizes leap shouting into the pool and dive with the speed of dolphins for each dinar thrown in by visitors. You should bear in mind children's nimble fingers when holding or opening your purse!

Carpet weaving in Gafsa

Adjoining the larger basin stands the palace of the former Bey, *Dar El Bey*, which now houses a craft centre with a sales counter. You can watch the women as they weave the well known Gafsa wall-hangings.

The inhabitants of Gafsa have laid out splendid vegetable and fruit gardens in its oasis, which begins immediately behind the Kasbah. Grape vines also thrive here.

 Hotel *Jugurtha*.

 By the *Lézard Rouge* (the train of the former Bey) from Metlaoui to the picturesque Selja Gorge (3 times a week).

 Office de Tourisme, Place des Piscines.

On the stretch of road to Gabès (about 30 km) there is a reserve for animals from the steppes and desert. Generally speaking you cannot see much without binoculars; the animals are usually too far away.

Useful things to know...

Before you go

Climate

The geographical situation of Tunisia, between the Mediterranean and the Sahara, results in areas of differing climates, thus making it a country to which you can travel at any time of year, with few restrictions in winter. There is no rainy period as such. The most frequent showers, which fall mainly on the coast and decrease as you move from north to south, are recorded in November, January and February. On the coasts, where the holiday resorts are, a cool sea-breeze produces pleasant climatic conditions even in summer.

What to take

The hotel shops in the holiday centres are quite well stocked, but nevertheless it is advisable to take your favourite cosmetic preparations, such as suntan lotions, and to pack the indispensable sunglasses.

Take enough films with you if you want to ensure you have the desired quality, as films are expensive in Tunisia. Smokers should take enough cigarettes; local 'black' cigarettes, similar to French brands, are produced. Mild Tunisian makes are *Good Luck* and *Yasmin*.

First-aid kit

All Tunisian chemists sell foreign — mostly French — preparations. However, you should take with you at least those medicines which you frequently use at home. In any case include the following in your first-aid kit: a pain-killer; a general antibiotic; a treatment for stomach and digestive upsets; an antiseptic for wounds and an analgesic for possible sunburn. Also pack tweezers for removing needles of cacti and sea-urchins. An insect repellent can also be useful.

All Tunisian doctors and chemists speak French; some speak English as well.

Health and Inoculations

Always check with your doctor regarding which inoculations are advisable or necessary well before departure date.

You are also recommended to refer to the DHSS leaflets: *The Traveller's Guide to Health, Before you go* (SA40) and *While you are away* (SA41).

Holiday Accommodation

The official hotel guide, as commissioned by the *Commissariat Général du Tourisme et du Thermalisme* in Tunis, is published annually. It can be obtained from the Tunisian Hotel Association in London (see page 93) and contains the following categories of hotels with the current average prices: ★★★★★ L = luxury; ★★★★ = 1st class; ★★★ = 2nd class; ★★ = 3rd class; ★ = 4th class.

Marhalas are rustically simple, but truly original, accommodation in old forts, oases or cave-dwellings. Examples are the *Campement Berbère*, Berber tents in Chenini, and the cave-hotels in Matmata and Ksar Haddad.

Youth Hostels are to be found in several Tunisian towns, including Gafsa, Monastir, Sfax, Sousse, Gabès and Kairouan.

Camping sites on the other hand are relatively scarce. 'Casual' camping is possible with the permission of the local police authority.

Getting to Tunisia

Although there are car ferries from Marseilles and Genoa, practically all visitors from the United Kingdom travel by air. There are regular services from Gatwick, the flight taking about 3 hours, and in addition there are many charter flights during the season.

There are international airports at Tunis, Monastir, Tozeur, Djerba and Sfax.

Immigration and Customs Regulations

Passports and visas: A valid passport or a British visitor's passport, obtainable from most post offices, is essential for entry into Tunisia.

Vehicle documents: A visitor bringing a private car to Tunisia must have in his possession a driving licence and registration document. For a stay of up to three months the Customs authorities will issue a vehicle permit exempting the owner from any duty, taxes, etc. The International Green Card should be endorsed as valid in Tunisia, otherwise the motorist will have to take out insurance with a Tunisian company on arrival.

Entry: In addition to normal travel requisites of a personal nature you are allowed to take into Tunisia free of duty: 2 cameras with a total of 20 films; 1 cassette player with 2 tapes; 1 cine-camera, 1 portable radio, 1 portable typewriter, binoculars, a child's pram/pushchair and sports equipment. In addition each person over 16 years of age can take: 400 cigarettes or 100 cigars or 500 grammes of tobacco. Alcohol: up to 25% proof 2 litres; over 25% proof 1 litre; 1/4 litre of perfume; 1 litre of toilet water, and gifts to a value of approximately £30. Video-cameras must be declared and will be entered in your passport.

You are not allowed to take weapons into or out of the country. Anyone who possesses underwater weapons renders himself liable to prosecution whether he uses them or not. There are special regulations relating to hunting-weapons.

Exit: Visitors can take out of Tunisia, without any formality, articles which they have purchased in the country for personal purposes.

It is forbidden to import and export Tunisian currency. On the other hand there is no limit on the amount of foreign currency (e.g. £ sterling or US $) which may be brought into the country. For large amounts it is recommended that you complete a currency declaration, the form for which you can obtain on arrival. You must provide this declaration if you wish to take out of the country at the end of your stay foreign currency worth more than 500 dinars (approximately £300).

Keep your exchange receipts because if you want to change dinars back into sterling when you leave you will have to produce those receipts, as only 30% of the sterling originally exchanged can be changed back again, with a maximum of 100 dinars.

During your stay

Currency

The Tunisian unit of currency is the dinar (D), divided into 1,000 millimes (m). In circulation at present are coins of the following denominations: 1, 2, 5, 10, 20 50 and 100 millimes and ½ and 1 dinar, and bank notes for ½, 1, 5, 10 and 20 dinars. In Tunisia you will pay about 60 pence for 1 dinar (at the time of going to press).

Tunisia is a member of the Eurocheque and Travellers' Cheques network. However, Eurocheques can be cashed only in banks. Many hotels and restaurants will accept credit cards.

Electricity

Generally 220 volts, with the exception of some older houses in Tunis and southern Tunisia where the voltage is 110. You are recommended to take a Euro-adaptor plug with you.

Newspapers and Books

British newspapers, periodicals and paperbacks can be obtained in Tunis and in all the larger holiday resorts. It is not worth having papers sent on to you. Printed post often takes 10 days.

Opening times

Mosques can normally be visited between 8 and 11 a.m., except on Fridays and during Ramadan. You are not allowed to enter the prayer rooms.

Unfortunately the opening times for museums, post offices, banks and administrative offices change frequently. At present the following apply:

Museums are closed on Mondays, but you can always visit excavation sites if you tip the overseer. Open: Oct. 1st— March 31st, 9 a.m.—noon and 2–5.30 p.m.; April 1st—Sept. 30th, 9 a.m.— noon and 3–6.30 p.m. During Ramadan: usually 9 a.m.—2 p.m. Bardo Museum: 9.30 a.m.—4.30 p.m. (closed on Mondays and official feast days).

Post Offices Sept. 1st—June 30th: Monday to Thursday 8 a.m.—noon and 2–5 p.m.; Friday and Saturday 8 a.m.— 12.30 p.m.; July 1st—Aug. 31st: Monday to Saturday 7.30 a.m.—1 p.m. During Ramadan: 8 a.m.—2 p.m.; Friday and Saturday until noon.

Banks Sept. 1st—June 30th: Monday to Thursday 8–11.30 a.m. and 2–5 p.m.; Friday 8–11.30 a.m.; July 1st—Aug. 31st: Monday to Friday 7 a.m.—noon. During Ramadan: Monday to Friday 8.15 a.m.— 12.30 p.m. Money can be changed on Sundays at the airports and in the hotels.

Government Offices: Winter 8.30 a.m.—3.30 p.m.; Friday and Saturday 8.30 a.m.—1 p.m. Summer 7.30 a.m.—1.30 p.m. During Ramadan approximately the same hours as in winter.

Shopping

You can shop everywhere from Monday to Saturday until about 7 p.m. Opening times depend generally on the climate; in summer the shops are closed for an extended lunch hour and keep open later in the evenings. During Ramadan they close before sundown, the end of the daily fasting period. Many, including some department stores and the shops in the souks, open again about two hours later and stay open until nearly midnight. Some stores open on Sunday and close on Monday.

Before you haggle in the souks for craft products you should obtain information about prices and quality at an ONAT (*Office National de l'Artisanat Tunisien*). All the larger towns have an ONAT. There you will find displayed everything that Tunisia has to offer from carpets, ceramics, leather goods and coral jewellery to kaftans and birdcages.

Time

Tunisia observes Central European Time throughout the whole year, i.e. one hour later than Greenwich Mean Time.

Tipping

Although a service charge is included in the bill, European guests are nevertheless expected to tip as well. In restaurants 5 to 10% of the total amount is the norm; in hotels waiters and room maids get about 1 dinar (60 pence) a week. You will be guaranteed royal treatment if you hand out a few dinars when you first arrive at the hotel.

Transport in Tunisia

Air Services

Tunis Air serves the Tunis — Monastir — Djerba route. *Tunisavia* flies to Tunis, Gabès, Sfax, Tozeur and on various minor routes and also hires out small aircraft with 9 to 50 seats.

Buses

Buses run between almost all the towns and villages. The fares are low but the buses are not well maintained. In Tunis the buses start from the Gare Routière.

Car hire

Cars can be hired without any problem in all tourist centres and large towns. All the international car-hire firms have branches in Tunisia. In addition there are purely Tunisian car-hire companies which are even cheaper. It is worth while comparing prices.

Railways

Trains run to the most important coastal towns in north and central Tunisia. Modern rolling stock makes the journey a pleasure. There are fully air-conditioned coaches, adjustable seats, light music and refreshments, but the trains are not particularly fast. In the cheapest class you can travel about 100 km for approximately 2.5 dinars (£1.50).

Taxis

Taxis are comparatively cheap, the basic charge being 200 m (12 pence), plus 120 m (7 pence) per kilometre; supplementary charge for luggage (night surcharge after 9 p.m.). If you wish to travel across country, shared taxis (*louage*) are to be recommended. They operate between all the larger places and can carry up to 5 passengers.

Important addresses

Diplomatic and Consular Offices

Tunisian Embassy
29 Prince's Gate
London SW7 1QG; tel. (01) 584 8117.

British Embassy
Place de la Victoire
Tunis; tel. 24 51 00.

Tourist Information

Tunisian National Tourist Office
7a Stafford Street
London W1; tel. (01) 499 2234

Tunisian Hotel Association
Reservation Office
1 Coleherne Road
London SW10; tel. (01) 373 4412

An embroiderer, Kairouan

Making yourself understood

Arabic and French are the official languages of Tunisia; visitors with a working knowledge of the latter will have no difficulty in making themselves understood. In the principal holiday areas English is also spoken at hotels, restaurants, etc. Below are a few useful words of Arabic, together with their meanings, which the holidaymaker will often encounter.

Abd: slave, servant (combined with the forename, e.g. Abd-Allah — slave of God).

Aid: feast or festival; *Aid El Kebir:* the Great Festival; *Aid es Seghir:* the Little Festival.

Ain: spring; *aiouina:* little spring.

Bab: gate; *Bab Souika:* gate to the little market.

Barra: shoo!, go away! (a loud shout to scare off children etc.).

Ben: son (often as part of the family name).

Bey: ruler (formerly the Turkish viceroy of Tunisia).

Bir: a well or fountain.

Bordj: castle, fortress-like building.

Chott: beach or salt lake.

Darbouka: hand drum made of earthenware.

Dar: house; *Dar El Bey:* house of the ruler (royal palace).

Djamaa: mosque, originally meeting place.

Djebel: hill, range of mountains.

Djellabah: cloak with a hood.

Djemel: dromedary.

Flus: money.

Foum: mouth, opening, gorge or ravine.

Fondouk: inn, guest house.

Ghorfa: room or barrel-vaulted storehouse.

Hadj: a pilgrim who has visited Mecca.

Hammam: Moorish steam-bath; *hamma:* warm spring (combined with the place name, e.g. *Hammam-Lif* a spa with hot medicinal springs).

Imam: prayer leader in the mosque.

Kadi: a judge.

Kaid: village head, tribal leader.

Kasbah: castle, also seat of government.

Koubba: domed mausoleum, pavilion.

Ksar: fortified place (part of the name in places such as Ksar Es-Souk).

La: no, not.

Malouf: tradition, custom (*Malouf* concert, folk music).

Machrek: the Arab East, land of the rising sun.

Maghreb: the Arab West, land of the setting sun.

Malesch: don't mention it! (in reply to an apology).

Marabout: burial place of a local saint.

Medina: old town, old Arab residential quarter.

Medrese (Medresse): Koran school.

Melha: Jewish quarter.

Mihrab: prayer-niche in the mosque facing towards Mecca.

Minarett: tower of a mosque.

Minbar: pulpit.

Mouloud: birthday of the prophet Mohammed.

Muezzin: the priest who calls to prayer.

Naam: yes.

Ouëd: river.

Ramadan: month of fasting.

Ribat: castle monastery.

Schurta: police.

Sebkha, Sebket: a small salt lake which often becomes a proper lake as the result of heavy rain.

Si — Sidi: master, lord (especially in saints' names such as Sidi Bou Said).

Souk: market.

Tabib: doctor.

Zankat: road, street.

Zaouia: memorial, shrine, prayer meeting.

Douz horsemen

Index

Original German text: Effi Horn. English translation: David Cocking.

Illustrations:
Pages 4, 7, 8, 15, 17, 27, 39, 42, 49, 50, 55, 61 (top), 64, 67 (top), 68, 73, 74, 83 (bottom), 84, 85, 93, 94, by courtesy of Tunisian National Tourist Office.
Pages 51, 52, 56, 58, 59 (top), 63, 76, 80, 81, Travel Trade Photography.
Pages 1, 5, 9, 19, 30, 34, 36, 45, 48, 53, 66, 72, 75, 77, Miss D. F. Goodrick

Series editor — English edition: Alec Court

© Verlag Robert Pfützner GmbH, München
Original German edition

© Jarrold Publishing, Norwich, Great Britain 1/90.
English language edition worldwide

Printed in Italy.

ISBN 0-7117-0466-X